TOUGH ENOUGH

HOW THE SUNS WON THE WEST

STAFF

DESIGNER
Diana Shantic

EDITORS
Tom Bauer, Greg Hilliard,
Kathy Tulumello

PHOTO EDITORS
Tim Koors, Michael Spector

PROJECT ADVISER
Howard I. Finberg

PROJECT MANAGER
Dave Gianelli

SPORTS EDITORS
Jeff Dozbaba, Don Henninger

REPORTING
Mark Armijo, Chris Cobbs,
John Davis, Norm Frauenheim,
Joe Gilmartin, Steve Weston,
Bob Young

STATISTICS
Greg Beihl

ASSISTANT PHOTO EDITORS
Mike Rynearson,
Rob Schumacher

PHOTOGRAPHERS
Credits appear on Page 120

COVER DESIGN
Patti Valdez

SYSTEMS MANAGER
Dave Seibert

IMAGING COORDINATOR
Joe Coleman

EDITORIAL ASSISTANT
Laurie Hagar

RESEARCHER
Donna Colletta

THE ARIZONA REPUBLIC/ THE PHOENIX GAZETTE

PUBLISHER
Louis A. Weil III

EXECUTIVE EDITOR
John F. Oppedahl

MANAGING EDITORS
Pam Johnson, Janet C. Leach

Charles Barkley awaits another
showdown with Michael Jordan after
his team loses Game 4 to Chicago in
the NBA Finals. Barkley led the Suns
to the finals for the first time since
1975-76.

I t's been a year for the books.

The Phoenix Suns, who hadn't won a conference title in 17 years, made a series of bold moves and put together a sterling season that should be remembered for its achievements and its unifying effect on the community.

That's why we've published this book.

It includes the best photojournalism from *The Arizona Republic* and *The Phoenix Gazette,* and illuminates a year in which Phoenix won the Western Conference, made a run at the NBA title and spread Suns fever throughout Arizona.

— **John F. Oppedahl**
Executive Editor

CONTENTS

THE BEGINNING   **11**
Another early exit means it's time for some changes

THE TRANSITION GAME   **13**
Surprising new faces replace one of Phoenix's favorites

THE TEAM   **25**
A new attitude arrives with the new season

THE REGULAR SEASON   **41**
Records fall as the team racks up 62 wins

THE PLAYOFFS   **61**
The Suns battle their way to a Western Conference title

THE FINALS   **89**
Phoenix gives heavy favorite Chicago a terrific struggle

Lack of sleep doesn't slow some of the 11,500 Suns fans **(next page)** who await their favorite team at 2:30 a.m. June 19 at Sky Harbor International Airport. Earlier that night, the Suns bested the Bulls in Chicago in Game 5.

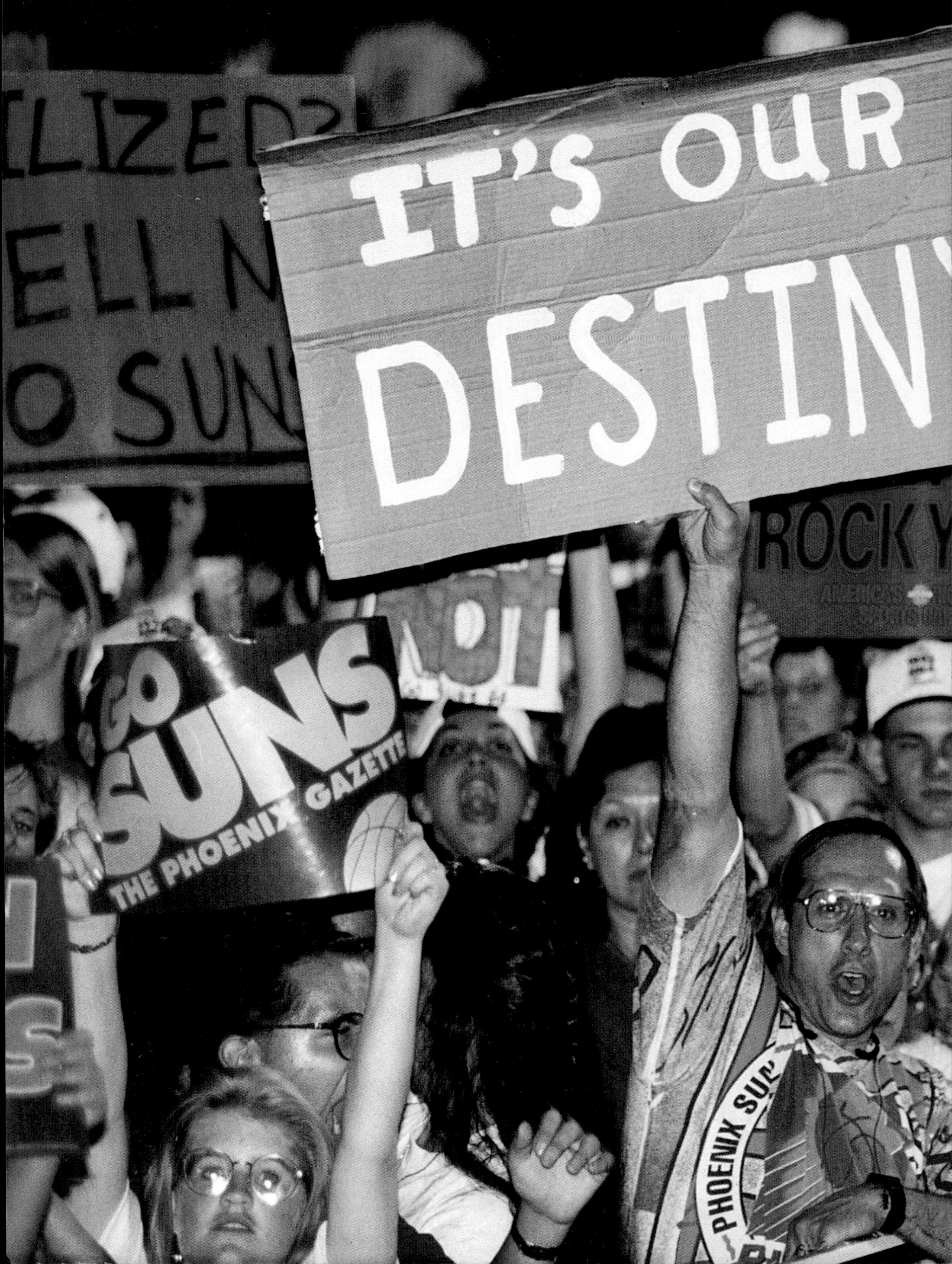
IT'S OUR
DESTIN
GO SUNS
THE PHOENIX GAZETTE
ROCKY
PHOENIX SU

Charles Barkley acknowledges the cheers from a huge airport crowd that firmly believes it is the Suns' destiny to win.

Coach Paul Westphal reminds the faithful that the Suns still have two more games to win after pulling out two victories in Chicago.

Kevin Johnson goes in for a hard landing courtesy of B.J. Armstrong and Bill Cartwright after Cartwright rejects a shot in Game 6.

Mark West and Horace Grant fight for position under the backboard in the final game. West had four rebounds and two blocked shots. Grant scored only one point, but his heads-up pass to John Paxson led to a game-winning three-pointer.

Sir Charles is king of the boards **(opposite page)** as he grabs one of his 17 rebounds away from Scottie Pippen.

Jerry Colangelo stands on the balcony outside his office at America West Arena, the state-of-the-art complex he's responsible for bringing to life. "I think we helped bring a community together — a community with a lot of differences," Colangelo says.

Shining hour for Suns chief

"I remember standing on the baseline in Boston Garden before the first game, waiting to be interviewed by CBS television.... I started looking at all those championship banners hanging from the rafters. I thought to myself how great it was to be there. And I remember thinking, 'We're here. This is just the first of many, many trips to the NBA Finals for the Suns.' Well, except for a couple of down periods, we've been one of the most successful franchises in the league since, and it has taken us 17 years to get back."

JERRY COLANGELO
Suns president

He had built this team. He had spearheaded the drive for America West Arena. But as he watched the Suns self-destruct against the Los Angeles Lakers, Jerry Colangelo wasn't thinking about the 62 wins or the Purple Palace or his pride in bringing the team into the league's elite after he and a group of local investors had bought it in 1987.

Colangelo, the Suns' president and guiding force, couldn't believe a squad led by Charles Barkley would let him down by crashing in the first round of the 1992-93 playoffs. And it didn't.

Weeks later, he could wipe tears from his eyes as the Suns earned a chance, in their silver-anniversary season, to win their first championship, and against the team that gave him his start, the Chicago Bulls.

TOUGH UNDER FIRE: Colangelo, who left the Bulls when he was 28 to become general manager of the expansion Suns in 1968-69, was named NBA Executive of the Year for the 1992-93 season, an honor he had won three times before, in 1975-76, 1980-81 and 1988-89.

Colangelo himself had proved tough under fire, trading perhaps the team's most popular player in 1991-92, Jeff Hornacek, to acquire the bad boy Barkley. He wanted playoff experience and a winner's attitude, so he jumped into the free-agent market to acquire Danny Ainge.

"We've always tried to be on the leading edge with our franchise, to be a model franchise," Colangelo said.

SEVERAL BOLD MOVES: When he took over as managing partner, he had a 54-game loser on his hands — a franchise ripped up by an over-hyped drug scandal. He hired Cotton Fitzsimmons and Paul Westphal and set about making bold move after bold move. One of the first was signing Tom Chambers as a free agent in 1988, which made the team an instant contender.

Colangelo had an earlier taste of the NBA Finals in 1976, when the Suns played the Celtics, but the intervening years made this year's visit sweeter.

"I've had a lot of lessons since," he said, "and it's why I appreciate this so much."

After the Bulls pulled out a finals victory, he said, "That's just the way it was meant to be."

THE BEGINNING

Jeff Hornacek leaves the court after the Suns lose to Portland. Hornacek would soon be the main cog in a huge Suns trade.

Cotton Fitzsimmons can't look as his Suns fall again.

It's May 15, 1992. The Suns end their 24th season with a 118-106 loss at Portland in Game 5 of the NBA playoffs' second round, and the next day's hailstorm of headlines would be familiar. *Too Soft. Not Tough Enough.* The Suns had heard it before. They had recorded four successive 50-win seasons, only to be outmuscled from the playoffs each year.

"We better go get us a Charles Barkley," assistant coach Lionel Hollins said as he walked off the floor.

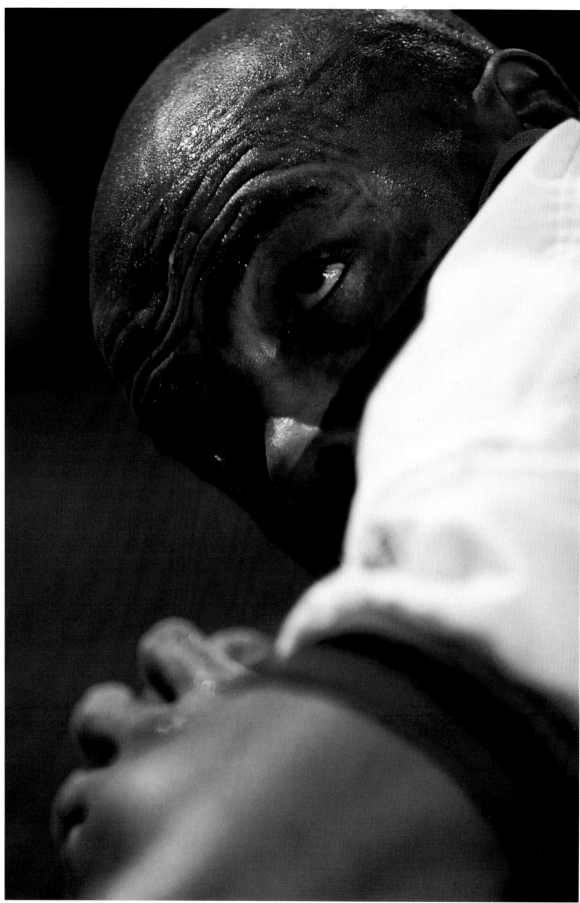

Charles Barkley quietly awaits his opportunity to wreak havoc on basketball courts throughout the West.

THE TRANSITION GAME

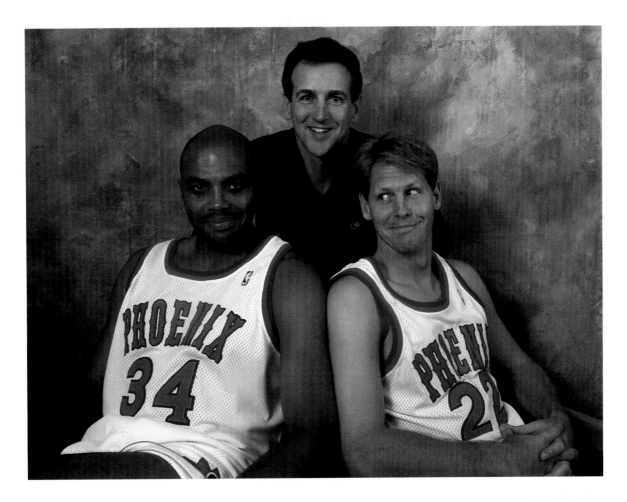

Suns President Jerry Colangelo set out to
remake his club in its silver anniversary season,
forging a revolution in style and substance.
New uniforms.
New, young coach.
New house, America West Arena. Listen to the
Purple Palace speakers rock and roll.
New warlord, NBA style. Sir Charles Barkley, the Beast
from the East, arrived, and suddenly everything else
was the B.C. era, as in "Before Chuck."

Outrageous! Suns deal for warrior

We need a Charles Barkley? Suns assistant Lionel Hollins could have been talking about a scaled-down version. Say, Charles Oakley of the New York Knicks. Or maybe Chuck Person of the Minnesota Timberwolves.

Each could be a Barkley. But the original edition? Never. Given the Suns' tradition for playing it safe and soft, Genghis Khan seemed a more likely acquisition.

So on June 17, 1992, much of Phoenix watched in wonder as Suns President Jerry Colangelo shook up everything, including his image as a conservative, close-to-the-vest businessman, by trading Jeff Hornacek, Andrew Lang and Tim Perry to the Philadelphia 76ers for *the* Barkley.

Hornacek was an Eagle Scout in a Suns uniform, a clean-cut family man who never uttered an angry word, helped old ladies cross the street and seldom missed a three-point goal.

"Phoenix isn't a bad place. I can play golf there every day."

CHARLES BARKLEY,
June 17, 1992

'DISRUPTIVE FORCE': Barkley had been acquitted of assault and battery charges in Milwaukee the same day the deal was announced. Also, his flight from Milwaukee to Philadelphia was delayed by a tornado warning.

"The omens are bad," angry talk-show crazies said. "Watch out."

Even a few of the so-called experts foresaw trouble. Barkley's arrival in Phoenix didn't alter the Las Vegas odds — the Suns were a 15-to-1 shot to win the NBA title — and Vegas Hilton oddsmaker Art Manteris, echoing an opinion held by many NBA observers, called Barkley a "disruptive force."

A disruptive force was the element the Suns had always lacked. A quarter-century without a championship was proof that you could not win without a so-called disruptive force. With one, there is always a risk of self-destructive dissension. But the Suns knew what the future held without taking that risk.

"Why not?" playmaker Kevin Johnson asked the day of Barkley trade. "You've got a perfect fit. You've got a contrast of colors, black-and-white stuff. Put it together, and it will work.

"Maybe we were too nice before."

Charles Barkley and Jeff Hornacek switched teams.

HISTORY OF BIG TRADES

OCT. 30, 1973: Connie Hawkins to the Los Angeles Lakers for Keith Erickson and second-round draft pick.

SEPT. 16, 1974: Neal Walk and a second-round pick to the New Orleans Jazz for Curtis Perry, Dennis Awtrey, Nate Hawthorne and a 1976 first-round pick, used to acquire Ricky Sobers.

MAY 23, 1975: Charlie Scott to the Boston Celtics for Paul Westphal and two second-round picks.

FEB. 1, 1976: John Shumate to Buffalo Braves for Garfield Heard and second-round pick.

JAN. 12, 1979: Ron Lee, Marty Byrnes, two first-round picks and cash to New Orleans Jazz for Truck Robinson.

JUNE 3, 1980: Paul Westphal to Seattle SuperSonics for Dennis Johnson.

JULY 7, 1982: Truck Robinson to the New York Knicks for Maurice Lucas.

JUNE 27, 1983: Dennis Johnson, first-round pick and third-round pick to Boston Celtics for Rick Robey and second-round picks.

FEB. 25, 1988: Larry Nance, Mike Sanders and first-round pick to Cleveland Cavaliers for Kevin Johnson, Mark West, Tyrone Corbin, one first-round pick and two second-round picks.

JUNE 17, 1992: Jeff Hornacek, Tim Perry and Andrew Lang to the Philadelphia 76ers for Charles Barkley.

Sir Charles opens season in the sun

Three days after he was traded to Phoenix, Charles Barkley stepped out of an open-air convertible and strolled into America West Arena for the first time.

The Ninth Wonder of the World, Barkley said.

Not yet, said Cotton Fitzsimmons as he pointed to the rafters. Retired numbers worn by Dick Van Arsdale, Connie Hawkins, Alvan Adams and Paul Westphal hang from the corners. There's a flag from the 1980-81 Pacific Division title.

But an NBA championship banner was missing. Fitzsimmons was quick to remind Barkley that he had yet to contribute to the building.

"You didn't put one nail in it," Fitzsimmons told him.

"I'm going to put up a banner," Barkley said.

"If you don't, what have you done?" Fitzsimmons shot back. "Nothing."

Cotton Fitzsimmons chauffered Charles Barkley into town, but it was Sir Charles who was counted on to drive the Suns to the play-offs.

Barkley has never been far from the spotlight.

Barkley gets a greeting and a challenge.

THE SUNS GOT...

Charles Barkley: A power forward, six-time All-Star, member of the 1992 Olympic Dream Team. In 1991-92 season, ranked sixth in the NBA in field-goal accuracy (55.2 percent), eighth in scoring (23.1 points) and 10th in rebounding (11.1).

Andrew Lang: An effective shot-blocker at center, but his offensive play in the half-court game was considered a liability. Averaged 7.7 points and 6.8 rebounds in '91-92.

Tim Perry: A defensive specialist who averaged 12.3 points and 6.9 rebounds in the '91-92 season.

Jeff Hornacek: A shooting guard who led Phoenix in scoring in 1991-92, averaging more than 20 points per game.

An elbow or two on road to victory

"When you get Charles, you get the whole package. You can't be selective. We all have warts, and in Charles' case, he's a great talent, a very competitive guy; he's outspoken and emotional. And a big part of his game is intimidation."

JERRY COLANGELO
Suns president

A basketball game for Charles Barkley is like a day at the beach for the United States Marines. He's always on the attack.

The world got a glimpse of his style during the Olympics, when he became the Dream Team's self-appointed ambassador of ill will.

Before the Games started, Barkley was asked about the rest of the field.

"Why don't they take their whippin' like people and go home?" he asked as teammates winced and diplomats scurried.

GOODWILL AMBASSADOR?: A day later, during a first-round game against Angola, Barkley delivered an elbow to the chest of forward Herlander Coimbra. A prelude to the elbow was a well-placed shove that knocked another Angolan out of bounds. The Dream Team was leading, 38-7, at the time.

Before the game ended, the fans in Barcelona, Spain, were whistling — not a compliment on the Continent — at Barkley. Magic Johnson and Michael Jordan they loved; Barkley they loved to hate.

Jordan was miffed. "If Charles would quit doing what he's doing, we'd get cheers instead of whistles," he said. "There's no place for it."

David Robinson was resigned. "Don't ask me about anything Charles does," Robinson said. "Charles is Charles. I can't speak for Charles. I can't control Charles. I haven't seen a person yet who can."

And Charles? Well, Charles was Charles. "It's a ghetto thing," he explained. "An eye for an eye, you know?"

The backcourt duo of Jeff Hornacek and Kevin Johnson never advanced beyond the Western Conference Finals.

Fans' favorite heads East

Jeff Hornacek thought it was a prank. The All-Star guard got a phone call from a buddy in Chicago who said he had just heard Hornacek had been traded from the Suns to the Philadelphia 76ers, along with center Andrew Lang and forward Tim Perry, for perennial All-Star forward Charles Barkley.

"I didn't believe him," Hornacek said. "I mean, my name really hadn't been in the papers, and nobody from the team had even called me."

The phone rang a few minutes later. It was Suns Coach Paul Westphal. What Hornacek had heard was true.

Hornacek, who averaged 20.1 points and had five years remaining on a seven-year contract worth $12 million, acknowledged he wasn't exactly prepared for the news.

"You always know there's a possibility you can be traded, but I wasn't mentioned in any of the rumors," he said. "I honestly had no idea this was coming."

FAMILY IN TEARS: He was one of the team's most popular players. Members of his family broke down in tears when they learned of the trade. A real-estate agent knocked on the Hornacek door at 9 o'clock the next morning to ask if he wanted to sell his house.

Hornacek threatened to retire and refused to attend a news conference in Philadelphia, but ultimately he and his family moved East.

"I blew it," he said. He meant that he had been with a Suns team that had a legitimate shot — or two — at winning an NBA championship ring but didn't do it.

Jeff Hornacek headed East, but he kept his house in the Valley.

Dumas leaps off-court obstacles

Before their resurrection, the Phoenix Suns were nearly wrecked by a drug scandal. But a player who battled his own drug problem became an exciting contributor in the 1992-93 season.

Acrobatic forward Richard Dumas had been selected in the second round of the 1991 draft, only to be barred from the NBA for the season when he failed a random drug test.

Dumas' drug problems had surfaced at Oklahoma State University, but the Suns decided to take a chance on him after Dumas played in Israel.

He was a standout in the Suns' rookie and free-agent camp and continued to impress the team in preseason camp before he failed the test.

"He's Dr. J with a jump shot."
JOHN LUCAS
San Antonio coach

"He would have been on our team," Suns Coach Paul Westphal said. "He's an all-around basketball player. He can shoot it. He can dribble. He's a good passer. He has good anticipation on defense. He has jumping ability, quickness and the talent to be a good defensive player."

THE ROAD BACK: The 6-foot-7 Dumas spent summer 1992 playing for the Miami Tropics of the U.S. Basketball League, then was reinstated Dec. 16 by the NBA.

The Tropics' roster was full of former NBA players who had been banned because of substance abuse. Former NBA star John Lucas, himself a recovering addict and now coach of the San Antonio Spurs, formed the team as part of his program for drug offenders.

Dumas proved the Suns' faith in him by averaging 15.8 points per game and being selected to the NBA's all-rookie second team.

"I really believe Richard matches up with anybody who was in the lottery except (Shaquille O'Neal of Orlando)," Westphal said.

Richard Dumas' skills drew rave reviews his rookie year.

Pounds hide tons of talent

The Suns are one of the deepest teams in the NBA, and few rookies can hope to make their roster.

Phoenix was fortunate in 1992 that Oliver Miller's stock dropped as much as his weight rose.

The Suns selected the 6-foot-9, 318-pound center from the University of Arkansas with the 22nd pick in the NBA draft's first round.

"But I'm in the mood to take a risk. Let's make (strength coach) Robin Pound earn his money. Anybody can get Kevin Johnson into shape."

PAUL WESTPHAL

Some among the 4,500 observers at America West Arena booed the choice.

"The last guy that received that kind of mixed welcome was Dan Majerle," Suns Coach Paul Westphal said, "so boo all you want."

Westphal was prophetic: Come the second half of the year, Miller was drawing cheers for his spirited play, just as Majerle did.

Before the draft, Miller said he would love to play for the Suns.

"It would be so great to play with Charles Barkley," he said. "I also think it would be a great opportunity for me because they traded one of their big men, (Andrew) Lang, to get Charles. I don't think I would be a starter, but I could come off the bench and help that team."

But before Miller could do that, he had to shed about 40 pounds.

Because of his bulk, Oliver Miller's skills were a mystery.

Danny Ainge, who never backs down from a challenge, says he craved more minutes at crunch time.

Ainge adds playoff savvy

The signing of All-Star forward and Dream Teamer Charles Barkley was clearly the biggest off-season move by the Suns.

But other acquisitions were needed to make the Phoenix machine run at its best.

Suns President Jerry Colangelo repeated one of his most successful maneuvers when he acquired 6-foot-5 guard Danny Ainge as a free agent on July 3, 1992. Four years before, the Suns had signed star forward Tom Chambers moments into the free-agent window, leading to the Suns' return to the elite ranks of the NBA. It was the league's first signing of an unrestricted free agent.

Colangelo said he first talked with Ainge "about an hour and a half or an hour and forty-five minutes after the (midnight June 30) deadline, and he officially was an unrestricted free agent."

Ainge's former ballclub, the Portland Trail Blazers, had made a two-year offer of $1.3 million to him and sat on it. But Ainge, a two-time NBA champion with the Boston Celtics, wanted a three-year deal in the neighborhood of $1.7 million a year.

A BETTER MOVE: Colangelo was more than willing to accommodate Ainge, signing him to a three-year contract worth $5.2 million on July 3.

Ainge, 34, said the Blazers overestimated his desire to remain in Portland, Ore., which is two hours from his hometown, Eugene. They gambled that family, friends and business interests in Portland would keep Ainge home.

"I was a little disappointed when they didn't call me Monday or Tuesday before the deadline," Ainge said of the Blazers. "When Jerry did call, it made it much easier to make the decision."

CHANCE TO PLAY: Ainge was unable to help the Blazers win an NBA championship, but the Suns and Colangelo thought that his veteran savvy would help the team in tight games and that his marksmanship with three-point field goals (40.3 percent for the season) would add another weapon to their arsenal.

Another concern for Ainge was playing time, and that changed in Phoenix, too.

"The one thing I said when I was in Portland was that I wished I could play more significant minutes in the fourth quarter."

"In Portland ... he was almost a specialist," Suns Coach Paul Westphal said. "We were counting on him to help replace Jeff Hornacek's shooting, but we didn't realize he could do so much more."

"He played baseball. He was an All-American quarterback in high school. He's a scratch golfer. Danny Ainge is the greatest athlete alive."

ACTOR JACK NICHOLSON

After Ainge's three-point shot capped an 11-0 third-quarter run in Game 4 against the Los Angeles Lakers, when the Suns tied the first playoff series, 2-2.

New arena, new season, new coach: Paul Westphal gets the blessing of his mentor, Cotton Fitzsimmons.

'Coach of future' ends 4-year wait for job

WHATEVER IT TAKES

Coach Paul Westphal has never taken himself or his job too seriously.

At the end of a close game, Westphal yelled in a play as his troops sped toward the bucket.

The play was ignored, but the Suns scored anyway.

Next time down the court, the coach frantically called for the same play. Again it was ignored, but again the Suns scored.

Westphal turned to an aide with a grin and said, "We fooled them. We made them think we were calling plays from the bench."

After four years as a sub, Paul Westphal finally became a starter for the Suns when he was officially tapped to succeed Cotton Fitzsimmons as head coach.

"I hope nobody is disappointed," Westphal told a news conference in April 1992.

Westphal's selection as Fitzsimmons' successor was not a well-guarded secret. The Suns were going to start their silver-anniversary season in a new building and with new uniforms, and the speculation was they would start the season with a new coach. Westphal had been groomed to replace Fitzsimmons during his four-year stint as an assistant coach.

"All I can say is, I have a tough act to follow," he said. "I wish anybody listening to me could have somebody as good ... to associate with in their professional life, or their life in general."

Along with the new arena and new

uniforms came the voice of a new generation: a former player who had served as Fitzsimmons' understudy but whose experience as a head coach was limited to a year at Southwestern College, a small Bible college in Phoenix, and two seasons at Grand Canyon College, where he won an NAIA national championship in 1988.

This followed an NBA career with stops in Boston, Phoenix, Seattle and New York.

NEW ATTITUDE: The new image is quieter, too. Fitzsimmons is famous for his motivational skills, which often meant yelling at his players. Westphal, on the other hand, encourages his players and makes games out of practices.

"As a player, one thing I hated was standing around," Westphal said. "I hated wasting time on things I already knew.

"And I didn't like practice just for the sake of practice when nothing could be

-Next page

Things have not always been peachy with Paul Westphal and the Suns.

Westphal has taken the team to arbitration twice over a contractual dispute, arguing that the Suns did not play him at the end of the 1983-84 season to avoid paying him a contract incentive clause. He lost both times.

The arbitration resulted in some bitter feelings between him and Suns President Jerry Colangelo.

"If six years ago you said I would be standing here as coach of the Phoenix Suns someday, I'd probably say that's very unlikely," Westphal said. "On the other hand, knowing the history of the relationship and knowing what, in fact, went down ... it's something that has made our relationship stronger.

"We said at the time it was more of a family squabble than an open war. I think families can have flare-ups, and relationships become stronger because of that."

Colangelo said time has healed the wounds.

In 1988, Westphal was named to the Suns' staff, and his number, 44, was retired. He was officially welcomed back to the family.

The sideline is quieter without Cotton Fitzsimmons, famous for his chatter with refs.

Paul Westphal is noted for his teaching abilities.

New era opens

-From previous page

accomplished but you had to practice anyway."

The players said Westphal's attitude has been rewarding.

Cedric Ceballos relaxed more with Westphal.

"He's excellent one-on-one and in teaching and making you excel without yelling and screaming, which is Cotton's way of motivating," Ceballos said.

"It's ideal for young guys like me," Negele Knight said after the summer leagues, "because he relates on a level that's more from the new school. He's fun to play for, because he's not afraid to try anything."

Cotton: Time for a change

Lowell "Cotton" Fitzsimmons, the gravel-voiced bane of NBA referees for 19 years, knew the time was right when he stepped aside as Suns head coach in April 1992.

"I thought it would be the right thing to open up the new arena with a new coach," he said.

Fitzsimmons was closing a successful four-year run with the Suns, his second stint for the franchise that gave him his start as an NBA head coach in 1970.

In between his Suns jobs, Fitzsimmons was well-traveled and occasionally fired, coaching in Atlanta, Buffalo, Kansas City and San Antonio. "Been fired twice, and both times they fired the right guy," Fitzsimmons likes to say.

Twice he was named NBA Coach of the Year: first in 1979 while at Kansas City and again in 1989 with the Suns.

He was the most successful coach in Suns' history, with a winning percentage of .638, but he knew it was time to move to the Suns front office.

"Paul is getting some gray hairs," Fitzsimmons said of his replacement, Paul Westphal. "I'd hate to see a man get old in front of my eyes and not be a head coach. ... It was nothing at all happening on the court. It was just time."

Despite leaving the Suns bench, coaching stays in Fitzsimmons' blood.

"I think (New York Knicks Coach) Pat Riley described me best," Fitzsimmons said. "He said I'm a lifer, and he's right. I'm a lifer. I was sentenced to life with no parole. That's me."

America West Arena became downtown's hottest new gathering spot. Fans flocked to see the new Purple Palace, which was in constant use.

■ *Overall, the arena has 1 million square feet of usable floor space.*

■ *Seating capacity ranges from 17,363 to 20,400, depending upon the event. Seating for basketball is 19,023.*

THE FINANCING TEAM

Phoenix contributed $35 million of the $90 million needed for construction of America West Arena. The city's share is financed by taxes on hotel rooms and on car and truck rentals.

The Suns, through their Phoenix Arena Development Limited Partnership, financed their portion of construction costs with proceeds from a bond sale arranged by the Maricopa County Industrial Development Authority.

The limited partnership will receive 60 percent of all revenues from arena advertising and luxury suite rentals. A large portion of the advertising revenue is to come from America West Airlines, which agreed to pay $26 million over 30 years to have its name on the building. Anything left over will be split 70-30 between the city and the partnership, respectively.

■ *About 175 people have full-time jobs at the arena; an additional 275 work there part time.*

■ *Each of the 88 luxury suites rents for $60,000 to $70,000 per year.*

There's no place like home

From the Madhouse on McDowell to the Purple Palace. Just a few miles down the road, but worlds apart.

Suns President Jerry Colangelo had arranged for his team to begin its 25th anniversary season in the new America West Arena, a $90 million, state-of-the-art facility at Jefferson and Second streets.

On April 16, 1992, the Suns bade farewell to Veterans Memorial Coliseum, their home for 24 years, with a win over San Antonio.

On June 7, 10 days before Colangelo closed his deal for Charles Barkley, 55,000 people showed up to tour the new arena. There was no event; the crowd just wanted to see the place. And all the seats had been sold long before Barkley arrived.

The Suns made their debut Oct. 18, and they delighted a sellout crowd with a 124-112 exhibition game victory over Boston.

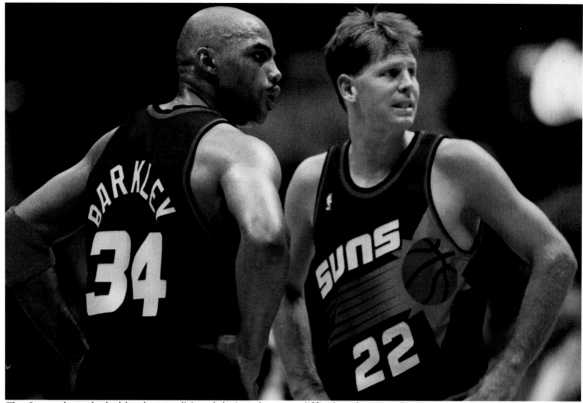

The Suns selected a bolder, but traditional design that was difficult to keep under wraps.

Shazam! A new look

Imagine Charles Barkley thundering down the court, the metallic orange and purple of his heavy-metal uniform shimmering like an AC/DC logo as he leaps for a dunk. Or how about Dan Majerle slicing through the lane in a uniform suggesting the style sense of Aztec Indians.

Both ideas flitted through the minds of designers working to come up with a new uniform for the Phoenix Suns, but the winning design was more traditional.

SECRET SLIPS OUT: Suns President Jerry Colangelo wanted the new look kept under wraps until Nov. 7, when the Suns met the Los Angeles Clippers in their first home game of the season. Along with a new coach and a new arena, the Suns would commemorate their 25th anniversary with a new look.

Bad idea. It's almost impossible to keep a secret. Ask any parent who has tried to plan a surprise birthday party with several children living in the house. Of course, the uniform cat got out of the bag.

Sportscaster Mike Chamberlin of KTVK-TV (Channel 3) received a copy of the 1992-93 NBA schedule in October, during the exhibition season, and when he saw the uniform tops of all NBA teams pictured on the cover, his eyes got big. He just

The Old West lettering was suddenly passe.

couldn't resist. Chamberlin waved the likeness of the Suns' uniform on camera, and soon everyone knew what the uniforms looked like.

THE TEAM

When Charles Barkley stormed into town,
there were questions. No, make that concerns.
Nobody in Philadelphia seemed to like him. Would
Suns forward Tom Chambers get along with him better
than '76er and former Sun Armon Gilliam had?
And what about Kevin Johnson? He was the Suns' star.
Barkley's aura was sure to eclipse KJ's and cast
Johnson into a supporting role. Could KJ handle it?
Nobody knew whether to dance in the streets or duck
into a shelter.

KJ shifts gears, assists team in different ways

aul Westphal had to shake his head every time he heard the suggestion early in this season that the Suns were just as good a team without Kevin Johnson.

"That's crazy," he would say. "Kevin Johnson is one of the best point guards in the league."

KJ became more of a true point guard this season.

With Charles Barkley now in the role of leading scorer, Johnson had to focus more attention on defense and playmaking.

While that was a challenge at first, he grew to accept and excel at it.

He also took on a tougher attitude, as witnessed on March 23 when his confrontation with New York Knicks guard Doc Rivers led to the worst brawl of the NBA season.

COSTLY INJURIES: "No one on this team has had to sacrifice their own game more," Westphal said.

"At every level he's played at, Kevin has been the main offensive weapon. He's the guy who did the scoring. Now he needs to do other things, and he's really handled it well."

If there was a downside to Johnson's season, it's that he continued to have injury problems with his valuable legs, keeping him out of 31 regular-season games (he was suspended for two others).

But he came back strong from a late-season knee strain that kept him out of the first playoff game.

His legs, when healthy, allow him to blow past opponents, penetrate the defense and score or open up opportunities for teammates.

He was sidelined early in the season, and the Suns got off to a torrid start without him.

NEED TO BE GREAT: No, the Suns didn't need him to be a good team. But they did to be a great one.

"To think I couldn't come in and make this team better is a foolish assumption by anyone," Johnson said.

When he did return, it took time to adjust to a new system and new players.

Once he accepted that the Suns were Charles Barkley's team, the adjustments were easy.

Off the court, he continued his good works, largely through the St. Hope Academy he founded in Sacramento.

It provides inner-city youths with opportunities for educational, cultural, spiritual and social development.

He was chosen as a "Point of Light" in former President Bush's 1,000 Points of Light volunteer-recognition program.

Kevin Johnson the playmaker helped push the team toward greatness.

	Games	FGs	3-FGs	FTs	Pts.	Avg.	Reb.	Ast.
STATISTICS								
92-93	49	282-565	1-8	226-276	791	16.1	2.1	7.8
Career	439	2835-5718	35-185	2379-2832	8084	18.4	3.3	9.7

Thunder Dan adds 3-point lightning

This year, Dan Majerle extended his game far beyond the three-point stripe.

Dan Majerle came full circle this year as a basketball player. Looking at his 1992-93 season, one might not guess that nearly all of his early playing days were spent in the paint throwing down slam dunks that earned him the nickname "Thunder."

It's not that the thunder has disappeared. Majerle still can go to the rack with the best of them.

But in the restructured lineup of Coach Paul Westphal, that wasn't where he was needed. So Thunder added some lightning, going from the paint to three-point land.

Watching some of the errant shots he launched five years ago as an NBA rookie, it would be difficult to predict that Majerle would lead the NBA and set team records for three-point shots made (167) and attempted (438). And it would have been preposterous to think he would set an NBA playoff record by making eight of 10 treys against the Seattle SuperSonics.

TRUE BELIEVER: Former Coach Cotton Fitzsimmons would tell you that he didn't have doubts. When Majerle was a rookie, he once missed a three-pointer with time running out and his team trailing by two points. Fitzsimmons stood by his player.

"Doesn't bother me a bit," he said, "because Dan really believes he can make that shot."

Many others, most notably the Los Angeles Lakers, came to believe the same thing this season.

In an April 6 game against the Lakers, Majerle nailed one three-point shot with 10.8 seconds to play that tied the game at 112. Then, trailing 114-112, he launched another from 33 feet that hit nothing but net as the final buzzer sounded, giving the Suns a one-point victory.

Most important, however, is that through the evolution of his game, Majerle's rugged playing style hasn't changed.

DESIRE, AND MORE: Early in his career, it was said of Majerle that he plays the game of basketball by two rules.

Rule 1: Every loose ball is his.

Rule 2: If the ball isn't loose, loosen it.

Hard-nosed? Chiseled.

Hard-bodied? He has the "Thundernine" calendars to prove it.

Hardheaded? He usually has the bumps and bruises and scratches to prove that, too.

We're talking about someone who once played about half of an NBA game with a separated shoulder. Trainer Joe Proski remembers that when Majerle walked past him to get resin on his hands as he always does after timeouts, he couldn't raise his arm.

"Most guys would have been out for the season," Proski said. Majerle missed nine games.

Right from his first NBA game in 1988, it was apparent that the Suns had drafted something they clearly lacked — a tenacious defender who would run naked through the underbrush if necessary to employ Rule 1 or Rule 2.

Defense, rebounding and hustle would be enough to keep Majerle in the NBA for years to come.

But he didn't stop there. Rather, he developed the kind of shooting and ball-handling skills that allowed him to become this season's starter at shooting guard.

Often, he still is called on to guard the opponents' best offensive player, but Majerle has become just as effective a scorer as he is a defender.

League coaches have recognized that in voting him to the Western Conference All-Star team each of the past two seasons. "If he's not an All-Star," Westphal said, "there isn't one."

STATISTICS

	Games	FGs	3-FGs	FTs	Pts.	Avg.	Reb.	Ast.
92-93	82	509-1096	167-438	203-261	1388	16.9	4.7	3.8
Career	368	1934-4200	330-914	935-1249	5133	13.9	5.2	3.0

DAN MAJERLE

Guard, 6-6, 220

BORN: Sept. 9, 1965, in Traverse City, Mich.

YEARS PRO: 5.

HOW ACQUIRED: 1988 NBA draft, first round, 14th overall pick.

RESIDENCE: Phoenix.

FAMILY: Father, Frank; mother, Sally; brothers, Steve and Jeff.

HOBBIES: Golf, weightlifting.

COLLEGE CAPSULE: Three-time All-Mid-American Conference selection at Central Michigan University. Averaged 23.7 points and 10.8 rebounds as senior and finished second in school history in points (2,055), steals (171) and field-goal percentage (.536).

PRO CAPSULE: This year was named to the NBA All-Star team for the second straight season. In 1991, was runner-up by one vote to Detlef Schrempf for the Sixth Man Award. Led the NBA in three-point field goals made (167) and attempted (438) in the 1992-93 season.

NOTABLE: Nickname is "Thunder." Set a Michigan Class A prep record by averaging 37.5 points per game at Traverse City and averaged 16 rebounds. Earned college degree in physical education. Active in the Valley's Stay in School program. Has his own line of clothing, Thundernine, some of which he designed, and popular Phoenix sports bar, Majerle's.

MARK WEST

Center, 6-10, 246

BORN: Born Nov. 5, 1960, at Fort Campbell, Ky.

YEARS PRO: 10.

HOW ACQUIRED: From Cleveland on Feb. 25, 1988, with Kevin Johnson, Tyrone Corbin and draft picks in exchange for Larry Nance, Mike Sanders and a draft pick.

RESIDENCE: Phoenix.

FAMILY: Wife, Elaina. Also has four brothers and two sisters.

HOBBIES: Travel.

COLLEGE CAPSULE: Averaged 11.4 points and 9.5 points in four years at Old Dominion. Finished as college basketball's No. 3 all-time shot blocker (446) behind Ralph Sampson and Tree Rollins. Led NCAA Division 1 in blocked shots two straight years.

PRO CAPSULE: The Suns' starting center hasn't missed a regular-season game in more than five years. Passed the 4,000 mark for career rebounds this season. Relying mainly on dunks for his points, led the NBA in field-goal percentage (.625) in 1989-90 and would have led in '90-91 (.647) but lacked the minimum number of attempts.

NOTABLE: Drafted in the second round (30th overall) by Dallas in 1983. Called "Big Daddy" by his teammates. Has college degree in finance and offers investment advice to teammates. Active in Arizona in working with underprivileged kids, donating his time for clinics and camps.

Hard-working Mark West battled big-name centers, like Orlando's Shaquille O'Neal, all year long.

West makes mark in paint

Flashy is not the right word to describe Mark West. He's not one of those NBA centers in the David Robinson-Hakeem Olajuwon mold who take over games with their scoring abilities.

But if you're looking for dependability and toughness, a true NBA iron man, West is a good fit.

Consider that he has missed only one game since joining the Suns, and that had nothing to do with an injury.

Shortly after coming to the Suns in the 1987-88 season, he was suspended for one game for an on-court run-in with then-Dallas center James Donaldson.

And even that year, he played in 83 games — one more than the regular-season number — because he had spent time with both Cleveland and the Suns.

ROLE PLAYER: This season, the 32-year-old West regained the starting job after Andrew Lang was traded to Philadelphia in the Charles Barkley deal.

West didn't miss a beat, fitting in as he always had, with a new roster of players.

Fitting in is something West knows he must do. While the term "role player" might indicate shortcomings in some circles, West doesn't look at it that way.

"I don't have a problem with that," he said. "I'm not in it for the hype as much as I am for winning. And I like to play basketball.

"Usually, teams that are very successful overall have good role players."

West worked hard during the off season, hoping it would pay off this year.

Not only did he work on his playing skills, he slimmed down to make himself more mobile.

"Big Daddy" or "Daddy," as his teammates call him, knows the Suns depend on him most to use his strength to defend the big centers.

And on the offensive end, he stays within his limits.

West consistently has one of the NBA's best field-goal percentages, although his shot totals don't qualify him for a ranking.

Knowing his limited range, he rarely shoots the ball outside of the paint.

"I think Mark always plays well," Coach Paul Westphal said. "His minutes aren't always consistent, so maybe it looks like he isn't consistent. But he always works hard."

Never were his abilities more appreciated than in Game 7 in the Western Conference Finals against the SuperSonics

He had a strong first half and scored 11 points overall.

West was considered the epitome of the "project" center when he played, sparingly, for Dallas, Milwaukee and Cleveland.

Many thought he wouldn't last.

"Here I am, regardless of what they say," West said. "I've been in the league 10 years and I'll probably be here a few more.

"So what I add to the team must be important."

	Games	FGs	3-FGs	FTs	Pts.	Avg.	Reb.	Ast.
STATISTICS								
92-93	82	175-285	0-0	86-166	436	5.3	5.6	0.4
Career	738	1951-3282	0-4	1000-1703	4902	7.5	5.6	0.4

Richard Dumas showed All-Star potential in his first year.

Rookie spells doom for foes

Probably no greater compliment a pro athlete can receive is one from his peers. So what did other NBA players have to say about the talents of Richard Dumas after getting their first look at the Suns' rookie?

"He's going to be a whole lot better than me," said Cleveland's Larry Nance, a former Sun and three-time All-Star. "Don't compare him to me. He's going to be his own player."

"He's a great leaper," said no less an authority than Atlanta's Dominique Wilkins.

Dumas did plenty of leaping and left plenty of impressions around the NBA this year.

Dumas missed the entire 1991-92 season and the first 19 games of this year after failing a random NBA drug test. He spent a year in a rehabilitation program run by San Antonio Spurs Coach John Lucas, and when he returned, it didn't take long to see why the Suns thought so highly of him. He came off the bench to score 16 points against the Lakers in his first game.

AERIAL SHOW: He climbed into a starting role, quickly became the Suns' No. 2 scorer and supplied some defensive aggressiveness at the small forward spot.

But mainly it was his high-flying dunks and alley-oop spikes that caught the attention of fans and opponents. He also was named to the NBA's second team All-Rookie squad.

But meeting the challenges Dumas faced on the court in his first NBA season paled in comparison to the ones he fought off the court.

"I think he's a grown up a lot," Coach Paul Westphal said. "I also think he's finding out that he's a much better player straight than when he was high."

GETTING A HANDLE: Understanding that basketball wasn't the most important thing in life is what helped him to overcome his substance-abuse problems, Dumas said.

While he had many offers to play overseas at higher salaries, Dumas opted to go through the rehab program and play for the Suns at the NBA minimum salary.

That convinced Westphal that Dumas was serious about overcoming his problems.

Lucas, who coached Dumas briefly with the Miami Tropics of the U.S. Basketball League, probably knows better than anyone the kind of player and the kind of person Dumas can be.

"Being able to play this game is never going to be Richard's problem," Lucas said.

"It makes me feel great when I see him playing so well. But it makes me feel even better to see him put his life in order."

STATISTICS								
	Games	FGs	3-FGs	FTs	Pts.	Avg.	Reb.	Ast.
92-93	48	302-576	1-3	152-215	757	15.8	4.6	1.3
Career	48	302-576	1-3	152-215	757	15.8	4.6	1.3

RICHARD DUMAS

Forward, 6-7, 204

BORN: May 19, 1969, in Tulsa, Okla.

YEARS PRO: Rookie.

HOW ACQUIRED: Drafted in second round (46th overall) in 1991.

RESIDENCE: Phoenix.

FAMILY: Wife, Angela; sons, Laron and Richard Tre III.

HOBBIES: Fishing.

COLLEGE CAPSULE: Played two years at Oklahoma State and had a 16.6 career scoring average. Was a freshman All-American and second-team Big Eight pick when he averaged 17.4 points and 6.4 rebounds. As a freshman, ranked second in the league in steals, fifth in rebounding, sixth in blocked shots and ninth in scoring.

PRO CAPSULE: Before this year's rookie season, when he became a starter, Dumas played one year in Israel and briefly for Oklahoma City of the CBA last year. In eight CBA games, he averaged 29.3 points and 8.7 rebounds.

NOTABLE: Attended Booker T. Washington High in Tulsa, where he was Oklahoma Player of the Year as a senior. Was suspended for the 1991-92 season for failing a random drug test and completed a rehabilitation program run by John Lucas, former NBA star and current coach of the San Antonio Spurs.

Charles Barkley, the league's MVP, coveted one more title: NBA champion.

A Most Valuable Presence

It didn't take long for fans to see exactly what was in store with Charles Barkley wearing a Suns uniform.

In the first game at America West Arena, an exhibition against Boston, he scored 27 points on 10-of-12 shooting, grabbed six rebounds and handed out five assists in 27 minutes. Then he was ejected.

Barkley — outspoken, controversial and talented — had arrived.

"I once heard a guy say that only one guy gets to be Elvis," Coach Paul Westphal said. "Only one guy gets to be Charles Barkley, and I think he's a good guy.

"He just doesn't go anywhere without attracting some attention."

BANNER YEAR: Barkley's dream year, which started last summer with his selection to the U.S. Olympic team, ended with a trip to the NBA Finals and with his being named the league's Most Valuable Player.

His explosive performance in key playoff games (43 points in Game 5, 44 points in Game 7 vs. Seattle) further proved his talent, and his heart.

The Suns gave up a lot to acquire Barkley from Philadelphia, but they never stopped believing they got the better of the deal.

Barkley was among the NBA's top scorers and rebounders all season, averaging 25.6 points and 12.2 rebounds. He also led the NBA in triple-doubles with six, and technical fouls, with 30.

And he provided the kind of leadership and intangibles that championship teams need.

"He gives this team leadership, credibility, you name it," Jerrod Mustaf said. "Plus, he's a comedian, a character. You have to take him seriously, but he keeps you loose."

Despite his controversial past, he was embraced quickly by the fans.

Halfway through his first Suns season, he was voted to its 25-year anniversary team.

A GOOD MATCH: Fans made him the leading vote-getter for the Western Conference All-Star team, and he made his seventh straight appearance in the game.

At the game, he wore jersey No. 23, which he requested because it was the number worn by Suns President Jerry Colangelo during his college days at Illinois.

"Jerry got me out of purgatory," Barkley said in reference to the trade. "I owe him a lot for that."

STATISTICS							
Games	FGs	3-FGs		FTs	Pts.	Avg. Reb. Ast.	
1992-93 76	716-1376	67-220		445-582	1944	25.6 12.2 5.1	
Career 686	5741-10098	281-1108		4365-5929	16128	23.5 11.6 3.9	

After sitting on the sidelines for much of the season, Oliver Miller played big in the playoffs.

OLIVER MILLER

Center, 6-9, 282

BORN: April 6, 1970, in Fort Worth, Texas.

YEARS PRO: Rookie.

How acquired: Drafted in first round (22nd overall) in 1992.

RESIDENCE: Phoenix.

HOBBIES: Reading, listening to music.

COLLEGE CAPSULE: Finished career at Arkansas as the school's all-time leader in blocked shots (345) and field-goal percentage (.636), ranking second in rebounds (886), sixth in assists (296) and seventh in scoring (1,674 points). Slowed by a foot stress fracture as a senior after leading the nation in field-goal percentage (.704) as a junior. That mark set a school record.

PRO CAPSULE: Missed much of this season because of injuries and problems keeping his weight under control.

O, yes! Miller worth the wait

Oliver Miller was the epitome of the term "weighty issue" this year. The 6-foot-9 center, with a weight estimated at more than 300 pounds, came to the Suns as a first-round draft pick.

Immediately, the wisecracks began flying. He was dubbed the "Really Big O" and "All-Over Miller." His basketball trunks were compared to the infield tarp at Candlestick Park.

Even his teammates got in their digs. When Miller was slowed by foot injuries early in the year, Charles Barkley said, "When you're that fat, your feet are going to hurt."

But the laughing subsided when it became apparent that Miller had basketball skills despite his considerable girth.

'FEEL FOR THE GAME': Opponents discovered that he still could get his frame off the floor well enough to block shots, and he could make remarkable passes.

"He can block shots, pass and score, and he wants to involve everybody," Kevin Johnson said.

"He's mentally and physically into it. He has a feel for the game. Larry Bird had a feel for the game. Some players just have it."

Miller developed that feel as a youngster when he used to watch former Lakers superstar Magic Johnson on TV, then try to imitate him in the driveway. His childhood friends called him "Baby Magic."

PASSING FANCY: When they lined up to play street football, his buddies knew what position Miller would play. Lineman? Forget it. He went for the glamour spot — quarterback, where he could throw the long ball.

He took those skills to the basketball court and the University of Arkansas.

When he left, he ranked first in school history in blocked shots, second in rebounds, sixth in assists and seventh in scoring.

But by his senior year, his weight had soared, contributing to a nagging stress fracture in his foot.

Those same problems followed him to the Suns, where he spent much of the first half of the season on the injured list until he reached the team's target weight of 285 pounds in early March, and his foot improved.

Barkley came up with the perfect slogan for Miller: "Lose weight, be great."

The rookie lived up to that promise with his overtime heroics in Game 5 of the first-round playoff series against Los Angeles, when he scored nine points, grabbed five rebounds and blocked a shot.

"Whatever it took, I was gonna do it," Miller said.

	Games	FGs	3-FGs	FTs	Pts.	Avg.	Reb.	Ast.
STATISTICS								
1992-93	56	121-255	0-3	71-100	313	5.6	4.9	2.1
Career	56	121-255	0-3	71-100	313	5.6	4.9	2.1

Fiery Ainge sharpens team's winning edge

DANNY AINGE

Guard, 6-5, 185

BORN: March 17, 1959, in Eugene, Ore.

YEARS PRO: 12.

HOW ACQUIRED: Signed as free agent on July 3, 1992.

RESIDENCE: Gilbert.

FAMILY: Wife, Michelle; children, Ashlee, Austin, Tanner and Taylor.

HOBBIES: An avid golfer, sports a 7 handicap.

COLLEGE CAPSULE: Scored in double figures in all 112 games he played at Brigham Young University. Was an All-American in 1981 when he won the John Wooden and Eastman Kodak awards as college player of the year.

PRO CAPSULE: Has played in NBA Finals eight times and has two championship rings with Boston. Also played in 1988 All-Star Game. Ranks third on NBA all-time three-point shooting list in both attempts (2,193) and number made (844).

NOTABLE: Played two seasons of major-league baseball with the Toronto Blue Jays, primarily as an infielder, and batted .220 in 211 games. Owns a line of hat shops. Actively involved with the Children's Miracle Network.

Danny Ainge has been called many things during his NBA career, and not all have been flattering.

He's been dubbed a whiner — even a crybaby — because of the way he curls his brow at officials. He's been called a "flopper" because of his ability to fall down and draw fouls on opponents.

But probably the most accurate label that can be pinned on Ainge is that of "winner."

Whether he's had to whine or flop or use any of the other tricks learned along his 12-year NBA trail, Ainge has won at nearly every stop.

Consider that this year marked the eighth time in his 12 seasons that Ainge has played in the NBA Finals. That's something few players can match.

And basketball isn't the only sport in which he's excelled. He's an avid golfer with a 7 handicap, and he played two seasons of pro baseball with the Toronto Blue Jays.

TEAM LEADER: But it was his basketball skills that the Suns went shopping for after they traded leading scorer Jeff Hornacek in the deal that brought Charles Barkley to Phoenix.

"When you think about the things we lost with Jeff and the kind of player you want to replace them with, you can't come up with anyone better than Danny Ainge," Suns President Jerry Colangelo said.

Ainge performed well, teaming up with Dan Majerle to set an NBA record for three-point shooting.

He also added the kind of leadership, intelligence and experience that help teams make extended playoff runs.

"In Portland, he played with bench players and was expected to carry them with his scoring," Coach Paul Westphal said.

"He was almost a specialist. We were counting on him to help replace Jeff Hornacek's shooting, but we didn't realize he could do so much more." Ainge is able to do more largely because of his strict off-season workout regimen. He stays healthy, too.

FIGHTING SPIRIT: Ainge has a knowledge and understanding of the game that make him a candidate to be an NBA coach. And he's never lost his competitive spirit.

"I don't believe there are limits to competitiveness," he said. "When players retire, what do they miss most? The competition. I, for one, will compete until I'm buried."

That is the kind of player Westphal wants in his lineup at crunch time, and Ainge was more than happy to oblige.

In his previous two seasons at Portland, he rarely found himself in the lineup with the game on the line in the final minutes.

"That's been the biggest difference," he said. "In Portland, I didn't play down the stretch unless somebody was in foul trouble. To be honest, it couldn't be more perfect for me here."

Nor for the Suns.

Danny Ainge thrives on playing with the game on the line.

STATISTICS								
	Games	FGs	3-FGs	FTs	Pts.	Avg.	Reb.	Ast.
1992-93	80	337-730	150-372	123-145	947	11.8	2.7	3.3
Career	900	4225-8975	844-2193	1493-1756	10787	12.0	2.8	4.2

Slam-dunk wizard Ceballos adds new defensive magic

Point-a-minute man. That's the nickname Cedric Ceballos earned in his rookie year with the Suns.

Figuring out why was easy. Ceballos has a knack for scoring in rapid-fire fashion.

Ceballos is most effective in a running style of game, with the ability to finish plays many others can't match. And he has always excelled on the offensive boards, where he knows how to score on put-backs.

But his role had to change somewhat this year, because Charles Barkley and other teammates also were racking up points.

"If he's not scoring," Barkley said, "he has to play well in the rest of his game."

Ceballos went to work on the other parts of his game after an early season home loss to the Chicago Bulls.

EARNED STARTER'S SPOT: Unable to even slow down Michael Jordan, Ceballos realized his skills had to expand if he was to be an effective small forward.

And while he's still not material for the NBA's all-defensive team, the effort he put into improving was duly noted.

"Cedric has gone from a guy who was just starting to a guy who has earned it," Coach Paul Westphal said in December.

Ceballos had to step aside as a starter midway through the season when rookie Richard Dumas exploded onto the scene.

But when Dumas went down with a severe ankle sprain, Westphal didn't hesitate to put Ceballos back in the starting role, and he played well enough to keep it after Dumas returned.

"I had other options," Westphal said, "but I didn't really consider anything else."

DUNK KING: Ceballos was a little-known player when he came out of Cal State-Fullerton as a second-round Suns draft pick, and 48th overall, in 1990.

He made a name for himself at the 1992 NBA All-Star game by winning the slam-dunk competition with his famous blindfolded dunk.

But his leaping skills and scoring abilities had become apparent to the Suns long before that.

They were skills he developed on the playgrounds of Los Angeles as a youngster.

"All the guys were bigger than me," he said. "I had to figure out ways to get the ball around or between their hands and do it quick.

"If you didn't, you knew someone was going to be coming up to block the shot."

Cedric Ceballos combined his familiar instant offense with new-found defensive skills.

CEDRIC CEBALLOS

Forward, 6-6, 210

BORN: Aug. 2, 1969, in Maui, Hawaii.

YEARS PRO: 3.

HOW ACQUIRED: 1990 NBA draft, second round, 48th pick overall.

RESIDENCE: Phoenix.

FAMILY: Mother, Rochelle; brother, Chris.

HOBBIES: Music and cars.

COLLEGE CAPSULE: Two-time All-Big West Conference player at Cal State-Fullerton. Led league in scoring as junior and senior, setting school record for career average (22.1). Was a junior-college All-American at Ventura (Calif.) Junior College.

PRO CAPSULE: Winner of the Gatorade Slam-Dunk contest on All-Star weekend in 1992. Made NBA history when he scored the Suns' 100th point in the first half vs. Denver on Nov. 10, 1990. Career high of 40 points came against Sacramento on March 9, 1993.

NOTABLE: Nickname is "Ice" but is known as the Suns' "point-a-minute man" because of his ability to score in quick bursts. Communications major makes many community-relations appearances in the Valley for the Suns.

The combined talents of Ceballos and Dumas created nightmares for opposing small forwards. "We have the same type of body and are both active," Ceballos said. "We're like a tag team, like a one-two punch."

Ceballos' season came to a painful end when he aggravated a foot injury in Game 6 against Seattle. The injury kept him out of the Finals against Chicago.

STATISTICS							
Games	FGs	3-FGs	FTs	Pts.	Avg.	Reb.	Ast.
1992-93 74	381-662	0-2	187-258	949	12.8	5.5	1.0
Career 201	761-1446	2-14	406-572	1930	9.6	3.5	0.8

Chambers flourishes in new role off bench

TOM CHAMBERS

Forward, 6-10, 230

BORN: June 21, 1959, in Ogden, Utah.

YEARS PRO: 12.

HOW ACQUIRED: Signed as unrestricted free agent on July 5, 1988.

RESIDENCE: Eden, Utah.

FAMILY: Three children, Erika, Skyler and Megan.

HOBBIES: Hunting, fishing and camping.

COLLEGE CAPSULE: Named first-team All-Western Athletic Conference and honorable mention All-American as he led Utah in scoring and rebounding. Is No. 6 scorer and No. 2 rebounder in Utah history.

PRO CAPSULE: Has appeared in four NBA All-Star games and was game MVP in 1987, when he scored 34 points. Scored 1,000 or more points in each of his first 11 NBA seasons and reached the 18,000-point mark this season. Set a Suns record in 1990 when he scored 60 points in a game against Seattle.

NOTABLE: Has been Suns' spokesman for the Cystic Fibrosis Foundation for the past five seasons.

This season was one of major adjustment for Tom Chambers. Once the focal point of the offense, the All-Star, the crunch-time go-to guy for the Suns, he became a role player, a bench player who performed in the shadow of Charles Barkley.

Many thought he couldn't possibly accept that role. After all, this is a player who had been an NBA All-Star four times, who once scored 60 points in a game for the Suns, who knew that whenever the team needed a big basket his number would be called.

But Chambers handled his new role like a professional.

Playing at forward and as a backup to center Mark West, Chambers provided offensive spark often for the Suns but had to focus his attention more on defense and rebounding.

"He's an important part of our success," Coach Paul Westphal said. "He understands his situation. He might not love it, it might not be his first choice, but he's enough of a professional to go along with it. It's noticed, and it's appreciated."

Chambers still could make any move or shot he had in his repertoire five years ago. He just couldn't do it as often, according to Westphal.

"In his prime, he was one of the toughest matchups in the league. He still might go out and score 35 if he played 40 minutes. ... But he couldn't do it consistently. There's no disgrace in that."

Chambers, however, believes strongly that his skills are intact.

"Teams still have to guard me; they can't leave me alone," he said.

TRANSITION GAME: Chambers, who makes his home in Utah, is one of those people who would rather spend his time hunting and fishing in the mountains and riding his horses.

In the city, he'd rather spend his time in the starting lineup than on the bench. But he knew that this year marked the best chance in his career to win a championship ring and that the number of chances were running out.

So he adapted without making waves.

"I could be a weenie about it and say this or do that," Chambers said late in the sea

son, before he was sidelined for nine games with an injured quadricep muscle.

"But this is a situation where we have a chance to win a championship. I'm not going to take away from that. I'm only going to try and help this team win."

SCORER'S TOUCH: In the playoffs, he gave the team a big boost in Game 7 against Seattle. Making his first start of the season, Chambers scored 17 points and grabbed six rebounds.

While he posted the lowest scoring average of his 13-year career, Chambers kept alive his career-long string of averaging in double figures and surpassed the 18,000-point mark.

When he was at center, he gave the Suns a smaller, quicker lineup that could run the floor and score from all positions. Barkley discovered early on that when he was double-teamed by opponents he could pass to an open Chambers, who maintains his ability to score.

"I enjoyed playing the other role (of starter and star)," Chambers said. "But it sure is fun to win."

Tom Chambers' desire to win a championship helped him accept a reserve role.

STATISTICS

	Games	FGs	3-FGs	FTs	Pts.	Avg.	Reb.	Ast.
1992-93	73	320-716	11-28	241-288	892	12.2	4.7	1.4
Career	933	6845-14541	207-668	4731-5852	18628	20.0	6.6	2.3

'4th-quarter Frank' beats odds

Suns Coach Paul Westphal didn't have any great expectations for Frank Johnson when the team invited the veteran guard to pre-season camp.

"We thought he'd come in, we'd take a look and he'd be gone," Westphal said.

"But he just kept hanging around and hanging around ... now we're stuck with him."

Johnson and the Suns were stuck with each other. Neither has a single regret.

The 34-year-old point guard became a key to the Suns' success, earning the nickname "Fourth-quarter Frank" for his contributions coming off the bench.

Actually, he was cut by the Suns near the end of camp and immediately contacted the Minnesota Timberwolves about pursuing a front-office job.

But the Suns called him back when Kevin Johnson suffered a hamstring injury.

"A lot of the guys told me when I left that I deserved to be in the NBA," he said.

ROSTER SPOT: Westphal agreed and kept him on the roster.

"We won a lot of games we wouldn't have won without him," Westphal said.

One of them might have been Game 3 vs. Seattle, when he scored 10 points in 13 minutes.

Johnson, who played at Wake Forest University, spent his first seven pro seasons with the Washington Bullets and then one with the Houston Rockets before he "disappeared."

Actually, he went to Italy and played three seasons. Though other teams around the league needed a veteran point guard, the Suns called first.

"Maybe the other teams didn't know where I was," he said. "They just kind of forgot about me.

"The other Johnson" — Frank — provided steady, aggressive play as backup point guard.

"I wouldn't have minded going back (to Italy), but I did want another chance to play in the NBA."

Johnson fit perfectly into the Suns' unusual triple combination at point guard.

Because he struggled in a bench role, Negele Knight was used mainly as the "second starter" when KJ was injured.

That put Frank Johnson in the substitute role for both, and he filled it well.

While he never posted dazzling numbers in the box scores, he was a dependable backup who used his experience to help teammates win.

SECOND CHANCE: His job was to keep the tempo high, play aggressive defense and help maintain leads while the starters rested.

Even if he doesn't play another year, this season is one he won't forget.

"To be able to come back to the NBA at my age after being out for three years, and to have this opportunity with a great organization like the Suns, is wonderful," he said. "Unbelievable, really."

FRANK JOHNSON

Guard, 6-1, 180

BORN: Nov. 23, 1958, in Weirsdale, Fla.

YEARS PRO: 9 NBA seasons, 3 in Italy.

How acquired: Signed as unrestricted free agent on Oct. 8, 1992.

RESIDENCE: Minneapolis.

FAMILY: Wife, Amy; daughters, Lidsay and Natalie.

HOBBIES: Golf.

COLLEGE CAPSULE: Averaged 16.2 points as a senior at Wake Forest University and was named to the 1981 All-Atlantic Coast Conference team and All-America second team by *The Sporting News.*

PRO CAPSULE: Averaged an NBA career-high 12.5 points and 8.1 assists for Washington in 1982-83. Averaged 10.7 ppg in '81-82, when he was named to the All-Rookie team. Played three pro seasons in Italy, for Rimini and Varese, before joining the Suns for the 1992-93 season.

NOTABLE: Was a first-round draft pick (11th overall) of the Bullets in 1981.

STATISTICS

	Games	FGs	3-FGs	FTs	Pts.	Avg.	Reb.	Ast.
1992-93	77	136-312	1-12	59-76	332	4.3	1.5	2.4
Career	526	1813-4134	51-231	936-1234	4613	8.8	1.8	4.4

Knight awaits his day

NEGELE KNIGHT

Guard, 6-1, 182

BORN: March 7, 1967, in Detroit.

YEARS PRO: 3.

HOW ACQUIRED: 1990 NBA draft, second round, 31st overall pick.

RESIDENCE: Phoenix.

FAMILY: Father, Willie; mother, Alma, is deceased.

HOBBIES: Music and movies.

COLLEGE CAPSULE: Named honorable mention All-American in 1990 when he averaged 22.8 points and a Dayton school record 6.8 assists per game. Finished career ranked first in school history in assists (663), starts (115) and games played (122) and sixth in scoring (1,806 points).

PRO CAPSULE: Was called on to start at point guard often this season when Kevin Johnson was sidelined by injuries. Missed half of 1991-92 season because of injuries after some impressive rookie showings. Was runner-up in Player of the Week voting in April 1991, when he started five games in Johnson's place and averaged 23.6 points and 11 assists.

NOTABLE: Led Detroit DePorres High School to 27-0 record and state title as senior. Received college degree in health education and has been a spokesman for the Arizona Dental Health Association the past three seasons.

Probably no other member of the Suns has a more precarious role than Negele Knight.

He became the No. 2 starting point guard this season, out of necessity.

When recurring leg injuries struck Kevin Johnson, Coach Paul Westphal had two choices for replacements: Knight and Frank Johnson.

He found that Knight was more effective as a starter and Frank Johnson excelled coming off the bench in relief of the other two.

"I think I do play better as a starter," Knight said. "But my style is different than Kevin's."

TRADE RUMORS: When Kevin Johnson was injured at the start of the season, Knight took over as the Suns won five of their first six games.

Later in the season, he struggled to regain his effectiveness after KJ went down with a deep calf bruise.

The problems were the result of spending many minutes on the bench, with Frank Johnson as the backup to KJ, and being the constant subject of trade rumors.

Ever since he came to the Suns, in the second round of the 1990 draft out of Dayton, other teams have had an eye on Knight.

This year, he was part of a trade package the Suns offered to Detroit for forward Dennis Rodman.

Knight admits the talk weighed on his mind, but he chose to look at the positive side.

Staying with the Suns meant he had a chance to play for an NBA title. Being traded probably would have meant more playing time as a starting point guard.

"It's tough to say, especially with a team like this," he said. "When you think about a championship ... that's a dream come true, and you want to be part of it.

"On the other hand, if your name is coming up in trade talks, you know you have value. I've seen other guys traded by the Suns, and they've gone on to do good things."

DIFFICULT ROLE: Being in the role of either starting or hardly playing is tough to accept. But Knight remained patient, something that's a whole lot easier when a team is heading to the NBA Finals.

"It's worth it," he said. "You're willing to do anything that's worth it, that has value.

"You just want to be prepared. You don't know what the future holds. I can't do anything but play. And if I can't play, then I'm not really doing anything."

After trade rumors proved unfounded, Negele Knight stayed for a chance at a championship ring.

	Games	FGs	3-FGs	FTs	Pts.	Avg.	Reb.	Ast.
1992-93	52	124-317	0-7	67-86	315	6.1	1.2	2.8
Career	158	358-842	10-45	171-252	897	5.7	1.1	2.8

STATISTICS

Jerrod Mustaf spent a lot of time on the bench as Charles Barkley's backup.

JERROD MUSTAF

Forward, 6-10, 245

BORN: Oct. 28, 1969, in Whiteville, N.C.

YEARS PRO: 3.

HOW ACQUIRED: From New York with Trent Tucker and two second-round draft picks for Xavier McDaniel on Oct. 1, 1991.

RESIDENCE: Chandler.

FAMILY: Daughter, Terah Kai.

HOBBIES: Reading, especially black history and current events.

COLLEGE CAPSULE: Left University of Maryland after sophomore year, when he led the team in scoring with an 18.5 average and was second in rebounding (7.7). Set school freshman scoring record with 14.3 average and had career high of 35.

PRO CAPSULE: Slowed by injuries this season after starting seven games early in year. Scored his NBA high of 19 points against Miami in 22 minutes on Dec. 26, 1991.

NOTABLE: Consensus prep All-American at DeMatha High School with selection to McDonald's, Parade and Converse teams. Favorite non-sports hero is Malcolm X. Hopes to pursue a political career when playing days are over.

'Moose' can't shake loose

Jerrod Mustaf became something of a forgotten man in the Suns' drive to the NBA Finals. It's not that difficult to understand when you consider a combination of factors:

As a power forward, he plays behind superstar Charles Barkley.

He spent the early part of the season on the injured list with hand and shin ailments, at a time when the Suns were laying the foundation for the season.

He still is one of the league's youngest players. Although this was his third NBA season, Mustaf is only 23.

In fact, this should have been Mustaf's rookie season. He came out of Maryland after his sophomore year.

EARLY START: While more college experience may have helped him early in his NBA career, Mustaf says he doesn't regret leaving early.

"People ask me that every year," he said. "I don't regret it at all. I was ready to move on, and I'm glad I did."

His top performance came in an early start against Charlotte when he scored 16 points and had five rebounds, one steal and a blocked shot.

When the Suns came out of fall training camp, Coach Paul Westphal's plan was to start Mustaf at power forward with Barkley at small forward as he had been in Philadelphia.

CHANGE IN PLANS: But it became apparent that Barkley would be more effective at the power spot with players like Cedric Ceballos and Richard Dumas flanking him.

That meant little playing time for "Moose," but it doesn't mean that Westphal has forgotten about the 6-foot-10 player who was drafted by New York in 1990. Mustaf was acquired by the Suns in a trade that sent Xavier McDaniel to the Knicks.

"He showed us a lot in training camp, and he's shown us at times what he can do in a game," Westphal said.

"I don't care that much about his scoring, and you can't ask him to do things he can't do. What we need from him is rebounding, and he can do that. He can be a big asset to this team."

STATISTICS								
	Games	FGs	3-FGs		FTs	Pts.	Avg.	Reb.	Ast.
1992-93	32	57-130	0-1		33-53	147	4.6	2.6	0.3
Career	146	255-551	0-2		138-211	648	4.4	2.7	0.3

Kempton goes along for the ride

Tim Kempton was signed as an insurance policy.

TIM KEMPTON

Center, 6-10, 255

BORN: Jan. 25, 1964, in Jamaica, N.Y.

YEARS PRO: 4 in NBA, 2 in Italy.

HOW ACQUIRED: Signed as unrestricted free agent on Aug. 18, 1992.

RESIDENCE: Orlando, Fla.

FAMILY: Mother, Mrs. Vincent Kempton.

HOBBIES: Golf.

COLLEGE CAPSULE: Averaged 8.6 points and 5.5 rebounds per game during his four years at Notre Dame, with scoring high of 10.6. Shot .516 from field and .786 at free-throw line in career.

PRO CAPSULE: Led Glaxo Verona to the Italian championship and European Cup title in 1991, making it the only team in history to accomplish that feat. Averaged 17.4 points in three seasons in Italian League.

NOTABLE: Drafted in sixth round in 1986 by the Los Angeles Clippers, where he played one season. Also played for Charlotte in 1988-89 and Denver in 1989-90. Was named to several All-America teams during prep career at St. Dominic High School in Oyster Bay, N.Y.

He didn't exactly tear up the NBA or make a run at MVP honors, but Tim Kempton had something of a dream year in the 1992-93 season for a couple of reasons.

One, he played for a team with the league's best record and reached the NBA Finals, albeit as a non-roster player.

Two, he no longer was the target of rock-throwing fans.

Concerned about Oliver Miller's weight and injuries, the Suns signed Kempton in August as a backup center to Mark West.

Kempton came out of Notre Dame as a sixth-round draft pick of the Los Angeles Clippers in 1986.

After that, he played two years in Italy, then one season apiece with Charlotte and Denver before going back to Italy for two more years.

In Italy, he learned just how ruthless fans could be.

In some places, he said, police had to escort players out of the gym, and fans followed the team bus for miles on the highway.

After one game in Sicily, the police failed to show up, and fans began pelting the bus with rocks, knocking out windows as players huddled on the floor with their duffel bags over their heads.

STAYED READY: Kempton took a pay cut for another chance to play in the NBA, where he didn't have to worry about dodging rocks and where he found little playing time with the Suns.

Kempton spent most of the season on the bench behind Miller, who became healthy enough to play, and Tom Chambers, who also backed up West.

But Kempton kept his role in perspective.

"Nobody promised me anything when I signed here," he said. "I knew the situation. Sometimes you're paid not to do something. My job is to practice hard, sit tight and stay ready."

KNOWS ROLE: Understanding that has helped Kempton survive in the NBA. Players who averaged just 6.5 points and 5.3 rebounds as a college senior and were drafted in the sixth round usually don't endure.

But Coach Paul Westphal says Kempton also understands the game.

"He's a basketball player," Westphal said. "By that I mean if he finds himself outside and they don't guard him, he'll make the shot. He can make the passes. He knows where he's supposed to go and what he's supposed to do."

Kempton also knows that he could have made more money or played more minutes with other teams, but he doesn't regret coming to the Suns.

"I wanted to come to a great organization," he said, "and one with a good shot at winning the whole thing. I've done that."

	Games	FGs	3-FGs	FTs	Pts.	Avg.	Reb.	Ast.
STATISTICS								
1992-93	30	19-48	0-0	18-31	56	1.9	1.3	0.6
Career	246	440-901	00-3	332-489	1212	4.9	3.1	0.6

Proski, Pound: Body shapers

For Joe Proski, the 1992-93 NBA season meant, among other things, the kind of training equipment he could only dream about in his early days with the Suns.

"We didn't even have a whirlpool," he said. "When I started, about all the equipment I had was a hydroculator, hot packs and ice — lots of ice."

That's a far cry from the facilities at state-of-the-art America West Arena.

Those facilities also were put to important use by Robin Pound, who completed his second year as the Suns' strength and conditioning coach.

Pound, 36, came to the Suns from the University of California, where he was strength and conditioning coach from 1987-91.

Among his big challenges this year was overseeing the dietary program of rookie center Oliver Miller, who lost approximately 40 pounds to get into playing shape and became a major contributor during the NBA playoffs.

Pound is one of the newer members of the Suns' family, but Proski has been an important fixture since Day 1, and we're not talking just taped ankles.

MANY DUTIES: Treating injuries, dispensing aspirin, handling travel details, taking care of equipment, keeping track of timeouts for Coach Paul Westphal and telling good stories all fall under the realm of "The Prosk."

He's been doing it for all of the Suns' 25 years, making him the longest-tenured trainer in the NBA.

Only three people — President Jerry Colangelo, his assistant Ruth Dryjanski and Proski — have been with the Suns for the team's entire existence.

"Yeah," Proski says with a smile, "me and Ruthie brought Jerry out here."

Actually, Colangelo brought the other two with him when he left the Chicago Bulls to become general manager of the expansion franchise in Phoenix.

Since then, Proski has been the trainer for three All-Star games and has traveled nearly 5 million miles. And he knows all about guys who can perform with pain.

After all, in the more than 2,000 games of the Suns' existence, he's missed only two of them.

Proski

Pound

Coaches add bench strength

One of the most important moves Paul Westphal had to make as new head coach of the Suns was one of the easiest.

Westphal didn't even have to leave the building to find his assistant coaches.

Lionel Hollins, a veteran of NBA wars and an NBA championship season, sat beside Westphal for four years as an assistant to Cotton Fitzsimmons.

Scotty Robertson, who had served four years as a Suns scout, knew all about sitting on that bench as a head coach and couldn't wait to get back.

Hollins, 39, and Robertson, 63, didn't hesitate to join the coaching staff that would lead the Suns to the 1993 NBA Finals.

Robertson's off-the-court passion is collecting classic cars. Hollins has an extensive collection of hats and caps.

What they did for the Suns was help collect victories.

"You know that's what I am — a coach," Robertson said. "I was a little surprised that Paul asked me in that our personalities are quite different, but he said that's one of the reasons he wanted me on the bench."

Robertson was the first coach of the New Orleans Jazz and later head coach of the Chicago Bulls and Detroit Pistons.

Even as a Suns scout, he often worked one-on-one with players.

STRONG-WILLED: Westphal saw Robertson's head-coaching experience and his strong will as invaluable additions to the staff.

"One thing I like about Scotty is that he's not afraid to tell you what he thinks," Westphal said. "The worst thing you can have is a bunch of yes men around you."

Westphal knew the kind of assistant he had in Hollins.

The former Arizona State All-American had played 10 years in the NBA and helped Portland win a championship in 1977. He was named twice to the league's All-Defensive Team.

Along the way, he learned valuable lessons from coaches like Jack Ramsay, Chuck Daly and Billy Cunningham.

He never lost sight of the importance of the basics.

"For me, X's and O's have always been simple," he said. "In school, instead of taking notes, I'd be writing down plays, football and basketball.

"When we went to practice, I always knew where everyone was supposed to be. I think that's how you win."

Hollins still puts that knowledge to use during Suns practices, frequently taking part in team scrimmages.

He also uses it in coaching the Suns' summer entry in the Rocky Mountain Revue, designed to give rookies and younger players more game experience in the off-season.

Like Westphal and Robertson, Hollins would like to be a head coach someday, but not at any price.

"If I'm never a head coach, I won't have any less satisfaction," he said. "I enjoy what I'm doing.

"If it's a good opportunity, I'd pursue it. But to be a head coach just to say I'm a head coach, my ego doesn't work that way. If nobody ever calls me and asks me to run their team, I won't lose any sleep."

Hollins

Robertson

PAUL WESTPHAL

BORN: Nov. 30, 1950, in Torrance, Calif.

FAMILY: Wife, Cindy; daughter, Victoria; son, Michael Paul.

PREP, COLLEGE CAPSULE: Starred at Aviation High School in Redondo Beach, Calif., and at the University of Southern California.

PRO CAPSULE: Drafted in first round, 1972, by Boston. Played 12 years as a guard in the NBA, six with Phoenix, three with Boston, two with New York, one with Seattle. All-NBA four times, NBA All-Star five times, Comeback Player of the Year in 1982-83.

COACHING CAPSULE: Began at Southwestern College, a small Baptist Bible school in Phoenix. Compiled a 21-9 record, and his 1986 team went to the National Little College Association Tournament. Spent two seasons at Grand Canyon College, where he had a 63-18 mark, winning the NAIA title in 1988. He was an assistant for the Suns for four years. In 1992-93, Westphal amassed a 62-20 record, the best ever by an NBA rookie coach. Coached West All-Star team.

He didn't whoop and holler much, but Paul Westphal knew how to motivate his squad.

'Westy' wins in relaxed style

Walk into Paul Westphal's coaching office and one of the first things you'll notice is a framed poster of one of sports' great philosophers — Sparky Anderson.

"When you get a group that wants to win," it reads, "you gotta let 'em."

Westphal had a group that wanted to, and did, win plenty in his first season as head coach of the Suns.

In fact, he's largely responsible for the team making its only two appearances in the NBA Finals — as a player in 1976 and as coach in 1993.

It was during that first visit to the finals that he displayed the kind of quick thinking and creativity that would one day make him an NBA coach.

Trailing Boston 111-110 with one second left in the second overtime of the fifth game of that series, he called for a timeout.

CREATIVE THINKER: Of course, the Suns had no timeouts left. Phoenix received a technical foul for calling it, and the free throw gave Boston a two-point lead.

But the Suns got the ball out of bounds, setting up Garfield Heard's famous shot from the top of the key. That tied the score and forced a triple overtime in what has been billed as the "Greatest Game Ever Played."

"He's one of the most creative basketball people I've ever been around," said Cotton Fitzsimmons, who turned over the coaching reins to Westphal at the end of the 1991-92 season.

That showed through at the end of the season when he designed a play that led to a bizarre Suns' win over Portland. Oliver Miller, inbounding the ball near midcourt with half a second to play, threw it off the back-board. Barkley scooped up the ricochet and flung it in the basket as the buzzer sounded for a 115-114 Suns win.

Most of all, Westphal is a coach who lets his players play.

He played 12 NBA seasons, was named to the All-Star team five times and never forgets what it was like being the guy taking the orders.

It might sound surprising, but it's probably true that the team with the NBA's best record this year is the one that practiced the least.

TEAM MOTIVATOR: Westphal doesn't hesitate to give the team days off when he thinks it's necessary. And when the Suns do practice, he turns nearly everything into a game in which winners are rewarded and losers pay.

"It's crazy when you think about it," he said. "We have guys who are making millions of dollars a year, and if I tell them to jog to the bleachers and back if they do something wrong, it motivates them.

"They're just a bunch of kids who started playing this game because they loved it. Despite the money and fame, the reason they continue to play it is because they love it. You play better when you're having fun, and you have fun when you're competing."

And there has been more than one verbal outburst during timeouts when Westphal thought his players weren't holding up their end of the deal.

Charles Barkley, for one, appreciated those displays.

"He can't worry about being our friend," Barkley said after one tongue-lashing. "We need a friend, we'll get a dog."

THE REGULAR SEASON

Sorry, Charles Barkley. You *are* a role model.
Not for kids, perhaps, but certainly for your
fellow players.
In January, perplexed teammates watched as you vaulted a
New York press table to confront the referees.
In March, they would have *followed* you.
KJ turned into an angry young man who said he was
playing with "a chip on his shoulder."
Even the fans changed. No longer were Boston Celtics or
New York Knicks jerseys so widespread in the Suns' home
that the players felt as if they were visitors.
As the team grew up, so did its fans.

BUILDING A WINNER

How the 1992-93 Suns players were acquired:

DANNY AINGE: signed as free agent, July 3, 1992.

CHARLES BARKLEY: acquired in trade from Philadelphia, June 17, 1992, for Jeff Hornacek, Tim Perry and Andrew Lang.

CEDRIC CEBALLOS: picked in second round of 1990 NBA draft (48th overall) from Cal State-Fullerton.

TOM CHAMBERS: signed as NBA's first unrestricted free agent on July 5, 1988.

RICHARD DUMAS: picked in second round of 1991 NBA draft (46th overall) from Oklahoma State.

FRANK JOHNSON: signed as an unrestricted free agent on Oct. 8, 1992.

KEVIN JOHNSON: obtained from Cleveland on Feb. 25, 1988, along with Mark West, Tyrone Corbin and draft picks in exchange for Larry Nance, Mike Sanders and a draft pick.

TIM KEMPTON: signed as an unrestricted free agent on Aug. 18, 1992.

NEGELE KNIGHT: picked in second round of 1990 NBA draft (31st overall) from the University of Dayton.

DAN MAJERLE: picked in first round of 1988 NBA draft (14th overall) from Central Michigan University.

OLIVER MILLER: chosen in first round of NBA draft (22nd overall) from University of Arkansas.

JERROD MUSTAF: obtained from New York Knicks on Oct. 1, 1991, with Trent Tucker (who did not report and was waived in November) and two second-round draft picks in exchange for Xavier McDaniel.

MARK WEST: obtained from Cleveland on Feb. 25, 1988, along with Kevin Johnson, Tyrone Corbin and draft picks in exchange for Larry Nance, Mike Sanders and a draft pick.

Dan Majerle, Danny Ainge and Charles Barkley were to play key roles in the Suns' development.

A new season, a new spirit

When the Suns acquired Charles Barkley, conventional wisdom said he would provide the toughness and physical presence the Suns lacked.

But could Barkley, a bona fide superstar, Dream Teamer and outrageously outspoken bad boy, co-exist with Kevin Johnson, the centerpiece of the Suns' four consecutive 50-win seasons?

Barkley and his teammates answered the question before the Suns played their first exhibition game.

PRESEASON CHALLENGE: Their preseason camp in Flagstaff was as physical as anyone could recall. When Barkley clobbered teammate Cedric Ceballos on a breakaway in a scrimmage, tempers flared.

Playmaker Kevin Johnson screamed, "That's weak, Chuck! That's bogus."

Danny Ainge, himself a Suns newcomer, also ripped Barkley for taking a cheap shot.

Later, Barkley admitted that he had been trying to goad KJ, who had shaved his head in the "Sir Charles" style for camp.

"I wanted to see how tough we were," Barkley said. "There were a lot of rumors that Kevin wasn't tough. He came after me. I like that."

A message had been delivered and returned. These Suns would be different. They would be resilient. They would fight.

QUESTION MARKS: Several other questions would have to be answered through the course of the regular season.

How would Tom Chambers handle being relegated to a supporting role?

Had the Suns given up too much of their interior defense in the trade for Barkley?

How would Ainge fit into the mix? The Suns signed Ainge to help replace Jeff Hornacek's perimeter shooting, but the veteran's minutes had waned in Portland. How much did he have left?

And would rookie center Oliver Miller, at more than 300 pounds, fit into the Suns rotation? For that matter, would he fit in a Suns uniform?

> *"If they'll fight me, that means they'll fight Karl Malone, Tim Hardaway, Shawn Kemp — the guys we have to fight."*
> **CHARLES BARKLEY**

Something to prove, KJ? Yes!

It began at the Suns' training camp in Flagstaff. Kevin Johnson, the team's point guard and resident philanthropist, declared that he would be a different guy in the 1992-93 season.

"You may even see me talking a little more trash out there," he said.

KJ? Founder of St. Hope Academy in Sacramento? Role model for children? Talking trash? It seemed about as likely as Charles Barkley taking a vow of silence.

But it was all part of KJ's intention to help Barkley transform the Suns into a tougher, more aggressive, and yes, occasionally nasty team.

THE INTIMIDATOR: If there was any doubt that KJ was serious about it, those were dispelled early in the season when the Suns engaged their old Western Conference nemesis, the Portland Trail Blazers, in a Nov. 25 rumble at America West Arena.

There was KJ, already with a technical foul under his belt, going after Portland guard Terry Porter after he was hit by a Porter elbow.

"I don't know why he was trying to be so physical," Porter said later. "It could be because they're trying to establish a physical presence with their team."

Pretty astute observation.

"When you have Charles Barkley on your team, you've got to go out and intimidate teams," KJ said.

So there KJ was again when the New York Knicks visited the Valley March 23 in a nationally televised battle of the Eastern and Western conference leaders. Just before the end of the first half, KJ nailed New York's Doc Rivers with a forearm to the chest.

It was retaliation for an elbow Rivers had thrown at KJ moments earlier. This time, a bench-clearing brawl erupted.

A NEW NICHE: It was emblematic of KJ's tumultuous season, in which he had to adjust to a new role with the addition of Barkley.

"Everybody knows I have struggled to find my role with this team," KJ said at one point during the season.

Although he surpassed Alvan Adams as the Suns' all-time career assist leader in April, KJ no longer was expected to carry the offensive load. Instead, he became the

Suns' defensive catalyst.

The adjustment was made more difficult by a series of injuries, which sidelined him for 31 regular-season games.

He missed the season's first six games after suffering a strained lower abdomen while helping Oliver Miller off the floor.

He sat out the final two games of the regular season and the first playoff game because of a strained knee injured during a celebration of Charles Barkley's game-winning shot in Portland on April 22.

But KJ returned for the Suns' second playoff game — just in time to knock Lakers' 7-foot-1 center Vlade Divac on his backside with a forearm. That prompted Divac to call KJ "a dirty player."

"They play in Los Angeles," KJ responded. "It's Hollywood. Vlade was probably trying to get a part in a movie."

KJ was on a mission to prove his status as one of the NBA's elite point guards.

Big O: 'I *do* have what it takes'

The Suns knew Oliver Miller was a gamble. Coach Paul Westphal said so on draft day, and at one point during Miller's rookie season, it appeared that the Suns might have rolled snake eyes.

In January, the Suns thought that Miller had trimmed down to 290. But on a six-game road trip to the East, opponents were driving by him with ease. How could this be if Miller were so much lighter?

TALE OF THE SCALE: The answer came when the Suns returned home to America West Arena and a new scale that had been installed during the road trip. This scale showed Miller at 323 pounds, far heavier than team officials had thought.

The Suns got tough. Because Miller was suffering from a weight-related injury (tendinitis in his right knee), the team placed him on the injured list and a crash diet, banned him from road trips, and told him he wouldn't return to the active roster until he reached 285 pounds on the new scale.

In exhibition season, Miller's game wasn't in shape.

"I'm working hard to get my weight down and my conditioning up, but it's a little more difficult than I thought," Miller said at the time. "Paul has stayed positive with me. As long as he's still on my side, I'll be OK."

Three workouts a day didn't seem to help.

"Nothing was working for me," Miller said. "I was to the point where I had to have some help."

NIGHTTIME FAST: Finally, Miller checked himself into Healthwest Regional Medical Center, where he spent his nights for several weeks. A sign on the door read, "No food in this room."

It worked. Miller, who went on the injured list Jan. 30, returned to the active roster March 10 against the Golden State Warriors after losing at least 41 pounds. At 282 pounds instead of 323 or more, Miller proved his worth, becoming a key factor as the Suns closed out the regular season with the NBA's best record.

His passing and shot-blocking feats brought to mind the criticism he'd heard from other teams before the NBA draft the previous June.

"They're all now sweating, looking at me play," he said. "I know a lot of teams wished they got me now."

The Suns were glad they were the ones who did.

"I'm just glad everyone kept their faith in me," Miller said. "I don't want to let anybody down. I want to show everybody in the NBA who didn't pick me that I *do* have a heart, that I *do* have pride, and that I *do* have what it takes to play in the NBA."

A slimmed-down Oliver Miller's shot-blocking skills frustrate Detroit's Isiah Thomas in a March 19 contest.

DEC. 30:
Tom Chambers flies ahead of Carl Herrera for a dunk in the Suns' franchise-record 14th straight win over Houston, 133-110.

NOV 7:
Danny Ainge's expression indicates he's met his mismatch against the Los Angeles Clippers' mammoth John Williams in the season opener.

FEB. 7:
Cedric Ceballos zips past Orlando forward Tom Tolbert in the Suns' 121-105 victory.

FEB 28:
Charles Barkley muscles his way around Cleveland's John Williams in Cleveland's 101-94 win. The Cavs won both games in the season series.

Suns trample records during yearlong run

The Phoenix Suns started the 82-game marathon that is the NBA season with a revamped line-up, a new playground, a new coach and a mission: reach the NBA Finals.

They did that, setting milestones along the way.

They compiled their best-ever record, 62-20, which led the NBA and locked up the home-court advantage throughout the playoffs. They ran off a team-record 14-game winning streak, which ended in controversy in San Antonio. (No matter. The Suns' road record was an NBA-best 27-14.)

Charles Barkley was named Most Valuable Player, cementing his standing among the top players on the planet. Sir Charles, no stranger to controversy, was suspended for a game after vaulting a table in New York to chastise a referee.

Dan Majerle led the NBA and set Phoenix records for three-point shots made (167) and attempted (438). Both he and Barkley were Western Conference All-Stars, Charles as the leading vote-getter and Majerle as a reserve.

CLOUDS OVER SUNS: But the long race had its valleys, too. The team went through several stretches without playmaker Kevin Johnson, rookie center Oliver Miller struggled with a weight problem, and rookie forward Richard Dumas went on the injured list with a severe ankle sprain.

Adapting to a changing lineup was difficult, too, as Westphal tinkered with his starting five even when all the players were healthy.

Being a fan in 1992-93 became a test of faith and nerves as the Suns maddeningly frittered away huge leads, although usually holding on to win.

Like the fifth win over hated Los Angeles, the first time the Suns swept the Lakers in a season series. The Suns blew a 20-point lead at America West Arena, winning 115-114 when Majerle hit a 33-footer at the buzzer.

PHILLY'S BAD BOY: The countdown to the season began with when it was announced June 17, 1992, that the Suns had traded Tim Perry, Andrew Lang and their beloved Jeff Hornacek for Philadelphia's bad boy, Barkley.

"Yeah, people used to say the Suns were soft, but we ain't that anymore," Barkley said. "Me and Danny (Ainge) have been working hard to get rid of that label."

Clearly, it was Barkley's year: from Dream Team gold in the Olympics to his 37-point home debut to his miracle shot against Portland after he caught a ricochet off the backboard with half a second left.

It got to where some people shaved their heads to look like Barkley. "Everybody wants to look like me," Sir Charles said.

No, Charles, but they all love to cheer you.

NOV 18:
Dan Majerle looks for room to shoot against Sacramento's Duane Causwell (left), Mitch Richmond and Wayman Tisdale. Phoenix won 127-111.

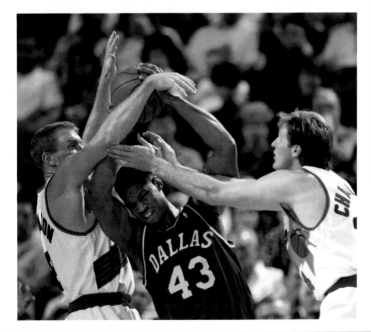

JAN 30:
Tim Kempton and Tom Chambers have Dallas' Terry Davis in a pinch in the Suns' 126-105 victory.

FEB 3:
Frank Johnson shields the ball during a drive into the lane against the Minnesota Timberwolves in the Suns' 122-102 rout. The Suns, however, frequently struggled against lesser opponents.

Count 'em: Spurs end run at 14

The Suns' record 14-game winning streak came to an ugly end Jan. 3 in San Antonio. In overtime.

The Suns blew a sure victory when the Spurs' Sean Elliott stole Dan Majerle's inbound pass in the final seconds of regulation and drove for a game-tying dunk.

If that weren't painful enough, the Suns argued that the Spurs had six players on the floor as San Antonio set up to inbound the ball with four-tenths of a second to play in regulation.

COUNTING TO SIX: Game tapes showed Majerle telling referee Joe Forte, "They have six! They have six!" Forte stopped San Antonio guard Avery Johnson from inbounding the ball and allowed the Spurs' J.R. Reid to leave the floor.

The Spurs went on to win in overtime, 114-113.

The Suns thought a technical foul should have been called and filed a formal protest.

Coach Paul Westphal conceded such protests are one-in-a-million shots but added, "I think this is the one."

It wasn't.

NBA Commissioner David Stern ruled 11 days later that the protest had been denied.

The Suns had argued that, based on the rules and the NBA casebook, Johnson had been given the ball and was prepared to inbound — a "live ball situation" under NBA guidelines.

QUIET, PLEASE: Stern ruled that it wasn't a live ball situation, and he referred to a casebook example of referee's stopping play before the ball is inbounded. However, the example Stern cited applied to a three-second violation.

"They just changed the rules of the game," Westphal said.

Had Majerle allowed the Spurs to inbound instead of notifying Forte, the Suns might have gotten their technical and extended the winning streak.

"I guess I screwed up twice," Majerle said. "First I threw the ball away. Then I opened my mouth."

FEB 7:
It was powerful, but it looked a lot like every other slam — until the basket support collapsed.

Workers hustle to install a replacement support so the game can continue after a damaging dunk by Orlando's Shaquille O'Neal.

'Shaq' brings down house

The newly christened America West Arena was still shiny and bright when 1993 Rookie of the Year Shaquille O'Neal arrived to vandalize it.

With 9:33 to play in the first quarter of the Suns-Orlando Magic game Feb. 7, the 7-foot-1, 303-pound superstar wowed a sellout crowd and stunned a national television audience when he snapped a $15,000 backboard support and literally brought the basket down with a power slam.

Jerry Colangelo, the awestruck Suns president, rose from his seat and said, "I've seen the glass shattered. I've seen rims torn down. But I've never seen the whole thing go."

O'Neal just took it in stride.

"It just happened," said O'Neal, who rated the dunk among his top five. "I'm going to continue to throw it down hard, and whatever happens, happens."

The game was delayed 37 minutes, after which the Suns returned to the court and beat O'Neal and the Magic 121-105.

O'Neal fouled out of the game, playing just 29 minutes.

He scored 20 points and grabbed five rebounds.

O'Neal enjoys the fruits of his labor.

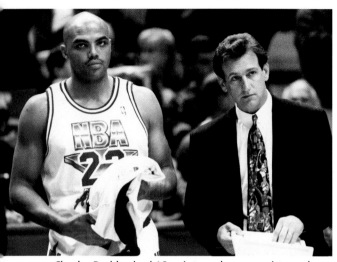

Charles Barkley had 16 points and seven assists, and Paul Westphal notched his first All-Star win as a coach.

Trio's work helps West play best

The NBA All-Star game on Feb. 21, one of the most competitive in memory, was a coming-out party that let the nation know the Suns were the Western Conference's new powerhouse.

Coach Paul Westphal became only the fifth rookie coach to coach an All-Star squad.

Charles Barkley led Western Conference players in fan voting and was in the starting lineup, playing most of the way at small forward.

And Dan Majerle's duel with Chicago's Michael Jordan highlighted the West's 135-132 overtime victory.

It was a classic matchup. Jordan, the league's scoring leader every year since 1986, vs. Majerle, one of the league's premier defenders. Jordan scored 30 points, but Majerle bottled him up at a crucial juncture, managed to score 18 points and nailed a critical three-point shot late in the game.

CRUCIAL MOVE: After Jordan had hit two driving layups against Portland's Clyde Drexler to give the East a 62-59 lead in the third quarter, Westphal summoned Majerle from the bench.

Jordan didn't score a basket the rest of the period.

"The people in Portland may not like me for that (substitution)," Westphal said. "I

just thought Dan was doing a little better job on him."

Westphal was right. Folks in Portland went nuts, and he was soundly booed nine days later when the Suns visited Portland Memorial Coliseum to play the Blazers.

But after the West's electrifying victory, a lot of basketball fans hoped to see a Majerle-Jordan rematch in the NBA Finals.

In June, their wish was granted.

Thunder Dan was a star on offense and defense for the Western Conference.

ROOKIE ALL-STAR COACHES:

1959: Ed Macauley, St. Louis Hawks, West

1978: Billy Cunningham, Philadelphia 76ers, East

1982: Pat Riley, Los Angeles Lakers, West

1991: Chris Ford, Boston Celtics, East

1993: Paul Westphal, Phoenix Suns, West

76er fans have nothing but cheers for their former bad boy.

The day before the game, Charles Barkley holds court in a hotel lobby for the Philadelphia media.

A Prodigal Sun returns

"To say it was difficult doesn't begin to cover it."

CHARLES BARKLEY
on his appearance
in Philadelphia

They came to say hello to Charles Barkley, and he said goodbye. "I am officially a Phoenix Sun today," Barkley said after leading his team to a 110-100 victory March 28 over his old team in the Spectrum in Philadelphia, where he spent the first eight years of his NBA career.

Philly fans gave Barkley a one-minute standing ovation at his introduction, then began booing when the lights were dimmed for the Sixers' introductions.

They brought their signs:

"Sir Charles is in the house."

"Yo! Welcome home, knucklehead."

"Now is Barkley's chance to shine."

As he stood on the free-throw line with 51 seconds left, a young man bolted onto the floor and hugged Barkley, who beamed broadly and talked to him.

"He said, 'I'm probably going to get arrested, but I'm happy to meet you,'" Barkley said.

When Barkley came out of the game with 18 seconds to go, the crowd began chanting, "MVP! MVP! MVP!"

The Sixers' front office must have wondered if it could have kept Barkley and solved its problems some other way. Obviously, a lot of people in Philadelphia would love to have him back.

But it's too late. He's a Sun now.

NOV. 7:
Mark West slips in for a dunk against the Los Angeles Clippers in the season opener. The Suns won 111-105.

MARCH 3:
KJ bites on a Jeff Hornacek fake in Hornacek's Phoenix homecoming, a 125-115 Suns win.

MARCH 23:
Paul Westphal disputes a call in the heated 121-92 victory over the New York Knicks that featured a bench-clearing brawl.

Signs and fans' warm wishes welcomed Jeff Hornacek in his only appearance at America West Arena.

'Jeff, Thanks for the memories'

When the 76ers came to Phoenix on March 3, Jeff Hornacek expected a warm reception. Even though he had been traded, the public thought of him not as a Sixer but as a Sun.

"I'll probably know most of the people in the first three rows. I should," Hornacek said. "We've talked with each other for years."

Sure enough, it was like old times. Actually, it was even better. Around the arena, from the courtside seats to the top row, members of the sellout crowd stood in tribute and cheered as Hornacek was introduced. Fans held up signs in salute.

"We Miss You, Jeff."

"Welcome Home, Hornacek."

"Jeff, Thanks for the memories."

The fans applauded whenever he scored and gave him a second standing ovation after he fouled out in the fourth quarter of the game, which the Sixers lost 125-115. He scored 15 points, making five of 12 shots, and had five rebounds and four assists.

It wasn't a spectacular return for former Suns Tim Perry, Andrew Lang or Hornacek. But then, Hornacek never was the flashy sort. Just hard-working, steady and willing to sacrifice whatever it took for his team to win.

These days, he does the same things for the 76ers — except now the wins come far less often.

Philadelphia Coach Doug Moe walks with Hornacek after he fouled out.

A fight sparked by Kevin Johnson and Doc Rivers grew frighteningly out of control.

Not in our house, Suns say

After all those championship years under the magnifying glass in Los Angeles, and two more seasons beneath the electron microscope that is New York City, Knicks Coach Pat Riley should have known better.

But there was Riley, in the aftermath of a March 23 bench-clearing brawl between his Knicks and the Suns that would set NBA records for suspensions and fines, blaming it all on the media.

"The whole thing was precipitated by a weeklong barrage of media coverage on the Phoenix Suns, about how soft they were," Riley said.

True, there were questions about how the undersized Suns had matched up against taller teams in the Eastern Conference, but the seeds were planted Jan. 18, when the Suns met the Knicks in Madison Square Garden.

NEVER AGAIN: Riley's Knicks — The Broadway Bullies, the club that wears its "tough town, tough team" motto like a tattoo — literally pounded out a 106-103 victory. The Suns complained that the Knicks were allowed to grab, hack, elbow and generally get away "with murder," as Charles Barkley termed it.

The Suns didn't forget.

When the Knicks arrived in the Valley for the rematch, the Suns were determined to fight fire with fire, and elbows with elbows, if necessary.

NOSE TO NOSE: By then, the Suns had the best record in the Western Conference; the Knicks were the best in the Eastern Conference. At stake was possible home-court advantage throughout the playoffs.

Tim Kempton restrains the Knicks' Anthony Mason, who confronts Oliver Miller.

Late in a tightly contested first half, the Suns' Kevin Johnson and the Knicks' Doc Rivers went nose to nose after an offensive foul was called on Rivers for an elbow.

KJ retaliated by leveling Rivers with a forearm just before the halftime buzzer. Rivers charged KJ, and both benches emptied.

And after KJ, Danny Ainge and the Knicks' Rivers, Greg Anthony, and Anthony Mason were ejected, they nearly went at each other again near the locker rooms. Security personnel had to step in.

The Suns got in the last punch. They beat New York, 121-92.

"The Knicks came in very, very tough," KJ said. "We had to respond. You can't let somebody come into your house and start moving stuff around."

"You have to give him credit. He must have a clothing contract. He could have ripped that suit or got sweat on it or something."

PAUL WESTPHAL

speaking of Knicks Coach Pat Riley after Riley jumped
into a bench-clearing brawl at America West Arena.
Riley ripped the pants of his Armani suit.

FEB 5:
Richard Dumas maneuvers through the Laker defense during a game in which he scored 24 points.

APRIL 6:
Dan Majerle slams his two-points' worth in the 115-114 win over the Lakers.

THE SWEEP

The Suns scored their first regular-season sweep of the Lakers in the 1992-93 season.

DEC. 4: Suns 103, Lakers 93
(America West Arena)
The Suns rode 50.7 percent field-goal shooting and 55 points from the bench to victory.

DEC. 18: Suns 116, Lakers 100
(Great Western Forum)
Charles Barkley's 25 points and 23 rebounds overwhelmed the Lakers.

FEB. 5: Suns 132, Lakers 104
(America West Arena)
Dan Majerle scored 29 points. The Suns shot more than 55 percent from the floor and led by as many as 34 points.

MARCH 24: Suns 120, Lakers 105
(Great Western Forum)
Barkley had 33 points, Danny Ainge had 27 and Tom Chambers 17 as the Suns built a 20-point lead.

APRIL 6: Suns 115, Lakers 114
(America West Arena)
Majerle hit a 33-footer at the final buzzer after the Suns blew a 20-point lead.

Dan Majerle can't believe it: His last-second bomb gave the Suns a 5-0 record against their perennial menace.

Lakers thunderstruck

KJ finds a Duane Cooper pass easy pickings.

The clock was winding down to its final tick when Dan Majerle launched a desperation heave 33 feet from the basket.

The clock expired before the ball fell through the hoop, but the shot counted and the Suns escaped with a 115-114 win.

Hollywood stuff from a Hollywood team, right? Wrong.

Majerle's April 6 shot let Phoenix post a five-game regular-season sweep of the Los Angeles Lakers, a first for the Suns franchise.

The Lakers were nearly as successful on the road as at home. Their road record, 19-22, was only one victory shy of their home mark, 20-21.

But Magic Johnson was gone, James Worthy was tired and Vlade Divac wasn't able to carry the team.

"We want to punish everybody who comes into our building," Majerle said. "It doesn't matter if it's Minnesota or the Lakers. It's our time now."

UP AND DOWN

Season statistics for Phoenix and Los Angeles

SUNS		LAKERS
62-20	Won-lost record	39-43
31-16	Vs. plus-.500 teams	18-29
31-4	Vs. minus-.500 teams	21-14
49.3	Field-goal pct.	47.3
75.3	Free-throw pct.	75.6
113.4	Scoring average	104.2
106.7	Points allowed	105.5
44	Rebounding avg.	41.4

APRIL 14:
KJ offers encouragement to Dan Majerle in a 98-84 victory against Minnesota, the Suns' 60th win.

MARCH 3:
An ex-teammate, 76er Manute Bol, greets Charles Barkley.

APRIL 19:
Cedric Ceballos' drive to the basket ends when he meets Houston's Otis Thorpe. The Rockets were the hottest team in the Western Conference at the time, and the Suns lost 111-97.

Even the Gorilla has gone commercial, appearing in chiropractic and pizza advertising.

Charles & Co. cash in on fame

Everywhere, it seems, there are Suns and more Suns, cashing in on endorsement opportunities that only a drive at a world championship can bring.

Charles Barkley out-dunks Godzilla, sings opera on the side and, we must assume, will be pitching something somewhere on the planet at any given moment. A few more Nike ads and Sir Charles will be worth more than Prince Charles.

Dan Majerle appears in commercials for Nike, McDonald's and a consortium of Valley Honda dealers. Cedric Ceballos, Danny Ainge and Kevin Johnson tout automobiles. Mark West talks about computers. Tom Chambers gets his back tweaked at First Chiropractic, and Paul Westphal really *does* eat at Whataburger.

'MARKETING GENIUSES': Whataburger has featured Suns head coach Westphal in TV spots since 1986, his first year as head coach at Grand Canyon College.

"We weren't even sure where Grand Canyon College was," said Mike Myers, operations manager for 36 Whataburger restaurants in the Valley and northern Arizona.

Westphal went on to win a small-college nation-al championship at Grand Canyon, then hired on with the Suns as an assistant coach and head coach-in-waiting. He brought Whataburger with him, Myers said.

"We started off with a small advertising package the first year, then moved on up," Myers said. "And then Paul was named head coach. It's just paid off 10 times more than our wildest dreams. Right now, we look like marketing geniuses."

GLOBAL PHENOMENON: Any discussion of endorsements, of course, must begin and end with Barkley, who in the past two years has developed into a global marketing phenomenon.

"Right now, you'd have to rate Michael (Jordan) and Charles right at the top," said Harvey Shank, who directs the Suns' various merchandising operations.

Barkley is Nike's point man of the moment, in heavier rotation than even the Chicago Bulls' Jordan, the company's darling for years.

Barkley's annual endorsement income "is well into the seven figures, just put it that way," said Glenn Guthrie, Barkley's business manager in Trussville, Ala.

"Charles has come a long way in the last three to four years, but everything really fell into place in the last 12 months," Guthrie said. "Things have flowed just like you would want them to."

Larger than life: Ceola Coaston, a secretary for the Phoenix Suns, busses Charles Barkley.

How much do we love our Suns?

Local TV ratings for Suns telecasts were at all-time highs throughout the year. On a per-capita basis, the Suns drew the best ratings of any NBA team.

The Suns drew 18,000 fans to America West Arena for a *practice* Dec. 21 — and had to turn away 3,000 at the door. The admission of $1 or one can of food netted 25,000 cans and $4,500 for the Salvation Army. The arena was filled again Jan. 8 for another practice and a party commemorating the Suns' 25th anniversary.

Five buses in Phoenix were painted with the likenesses of Charles Barkley, Dan Majerle, Kevin Johnson, Tom Chambers and the Gorilla.

Bank of America lured more than 30,000 new customers by offering Suns Checking, featuring orange checks and purple checkbook covers.

Subway reported heavy demand for $1 Suns/Subway water bottles: 50,000 bottles were ordered in February, and an additional 56,000 were ordered in April.

Sales of Suns merchandise ranked among the top five in the NBA. Fans could choose from a bewildering selection of T-shirts, sweat shirts, jackets, warm-ups, watches, mugs, posters, books, videos and hundreds of other items. The No. 1 item of conspicuous consumption was a $4,000 leather jacket featuring the autographs of several players.

A downtown bar and grill operated by Dan Majerle was packing in 1,000 customers a day. Many customers would show up three hours before the start of a Suns telecast to claim a table.

THE PLAYOFFS

Whew, that was close. It looked like the old
Phoenix Softies had reappeared. The Lakers beat the Suns
in the America West fortress in the playoffs'
first two games. But not to worry.
Coach Paul Westphal boldly promised to prevail,
guaranteeing three successive victories. Westphal's troops
delivered, but only with flu-ridden Dan Majerle sinking a
jumper in the closing seconds of the decisive fifth game.
It was as if the Suns wanted to look over the edge and into
the deep, dark despair of a bygone era just so they could
prove they were tough enough.
They were.

ROUND 1: LAKERS

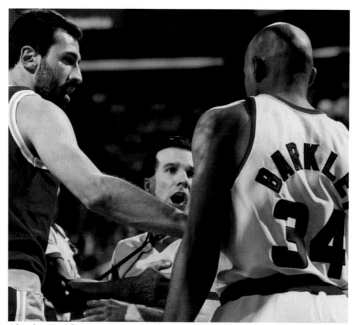

GAME 1 The team with the NBA's best record welcomed the playoff contender with the worst one and received a slap in the face.

The Suns and Lakers kicked off the 1993 Western Conference playoffs in Phoenix on April 30. Los Angeles' Sedale Threatt scored 35 points. The shellshocked Suns failed to score on all seven possessions in the final 2:41 as the Lakers won Game 1 in the best-of-five series, 107-103.

"Our team played smart and kept its poise," Lakers Coach Randy Pfund said. "That is what you have to do at this time of year."

The Suns, playing without injured point guard Kevin Johnson, were led by Charles Barkley's 34 points and 15 rebounds.

"It was pretty simple: They played playoff basketball, and we didn't," Suns Coach Paul Westphal said.

Charles Barkley receives a technical foul as Vlade Divac gives his opinion during Game 1.

LAKERS 107, SUNS 103

LA LAKERS

	Mn	FG	FT	Rb	At	PF	St	Tr	Pt
Campbell f	32	4-10	1-4	9	2	4	1	2	9
Green f	39	4- 6	0-0	9	3	2	1	1	8
Divac c	37	5-9	2-4	10	6	5	2	3	12
Scott g	35	6-11	9-11	2	2	0	2	0	22
Threatt g	40	17-24	1- 2	3	7	3	3	3	35
Worthy	31	4-15	1-2	5	4	3	0	2	9
Christie	8	2-3	0-0	1	1	0	1	2	4
Smith	13	2-4	2-2	1	0	3	0	1	6
Edwards	5	1-1	0-0	2	0	0	0	0	2
Totals		**45-83**	**16-25**	**42**	**25**	**20**	**10**	**11**	**107**

PHOENIX

	Mn	FG	FT	Rb	At	PF	St	Tr	Pt
Ceballos f	26	3- 9	0-0	6	4	1	1	1	6
Barkley f	44	12-16	10-15	15	4	2	2	2	34
West c	22	4-8	0-0	5	0	3	0	0	8
Knight g	21	5-9	0-0	3	5	1	0	1	10
Majerle g	48	4-15	1-2	3	5	4	0	1	9
Chambers	28	7-11	4-4	5	3	5	1	4	18
Dumas	16	3-6	0-0	1	1	2	1	1	6
Ainge	27	4-13	1-1	1	2	3	2	1	10
Miller	4	0-0	0-0	0	2	0	0	2	0
F.Johnson	4	1-2	0-0	0	0	1	0	0	2
Totals		**43-89**	**16-22**	**39**	**26**	**22**	**7**	**13**	**103**

FG percentage: LA Lakers .542, Phoenix .483.
FT percentage: LA Lakers .640, Phoenix .727.
Three-point shots: LA Lakers 1-4 (Scott 1-2, Threatt 0-1, Worthy 0-1),Phoenix 1-11 (Ainge 1-5, Majerle 0-6). **Blocked shots:** LA Lakers 6 (Campbell 3, Divac, Christie, Smith), Phoenix 3 (Barkley 2, West). **Technicals:** Barkley, Campbell.

LA LAKERS	27	26	30	24	107
PHOENIX	33	13	33	24	103

Officials: Ed T. Rush, Jack Nies and Ken Mauer.
Attendance: 19,023.
Time: 2:19.

Kevin Johnson drives against A.C. Green with the season on the line in Game 5.

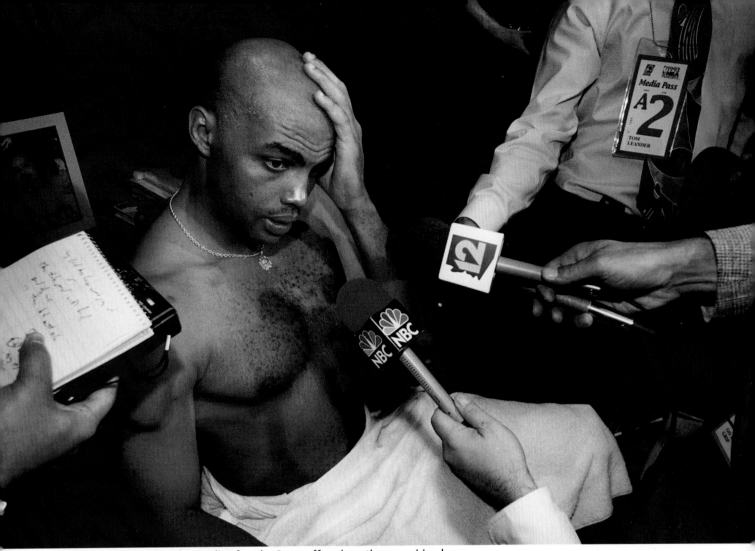

Charles Barkley is confronted by the media after the Suns suffered another surprising loss.

Mark West (left) and Cedric Ceballos scramble for the ball.

GAME 2 Many so-called experts thought the Suns would win three straight against the Lakers — and after losing 86-81 to Los Angeles at America West Arena on May 2, the Suns would have to.

Shooting only 42 percent and scoring a franchise playoff-low 11 points in the fourth quarter, the Suns found themselves down 0-2 in the series. Another loss and the Suns would make NBA history by becoming the loftiest team to be defeated by the lowliest team.

Charles Barkley missed all seven of his fourth-quarter shots and made only eight of 24 overall.

"I picked a bad time to have my worst game of the year," Barkley said. "I'm just disappointed."

Even the Lakers seemed surprised by their success.

"If somebody had told me that we'd be 2-0 in this one," Laker center Vlade Divac said, "I would have looked at him and said, 'You are very, very crazy.'"

LAKERS 86, SUNS 81

LA LAKERS

	Mn	FG	FT	Rb	At	PF	St	Tr	Pt
Campbell f	41	6-15	3-4	8	3	1	1	3	15
Green f	42	1-5	5-8	13	3	2	2	2	7
Divac c	34	8-15	2-7	13	6	3	1	5	19
Scott g	30	7-10	0-2	1	2	5	0	1	17
Threatt g	43	4-14	0-0	6	8	4	3	2	9
Worthy	24	5-14	0-0	2	2	2	0	0	11
Edwards	3	1-1	0-0	0	0	2	0	1	2
Christie	5	0-1	0-0	0	0	2	0	1	0
Smith	18	3-4	0-2	3	1	2	0	1	6
Totals		**35-79**	**10-23**	**46**	**25**	**23**	**7**	**16**	**86**

PHOENIX

	Mn	FG	FT	Rb	At	PF	St	Tr	Pt
Barkley f	44	8-24	2-4	21	3	4	1	1	18
Dumas f	24	7-11	4-8	3	2	1	0	0	18
West c	23	1-2	1-2	6	0	3	0	1	3
KJohnson g	44	6-10	2-2	1	16	2	2	5	14
Majerle g	40	3-11	1-2	3	1	5	4	1	8
Miller	10	0-1	0-0	2	1	2	0	3	0
Chambers	31	8-15	2-3	1	0	2	0	2	18
Ainge	20	1-7	0-0	4	1	0	0	0	2
Ceballos	4	0-0	0-0	1	0	1	0	0	0
Totals		**34-81**	**12-21**	**42**	**24**	**20**	**7**	**13**	**81**

FG percentage: LA Lakers .443, Phoenix .420.
FT percentage: LA Lakers .435, Phoenix .571.
Three-point shots: LA Lakers 6-13 (Scott 3-5, Threatt 1-4, Worthy 1-3, Divac 1-1), Phoenix 1-8 (Majerle 1-5, Ainge 0-2, Dumas 0-1). **Blocked shots:** LA Lakers 7 (Campbell 3, Divac 3, Christie), Phoenix 2 (Miller, Chambers). **Technicals:** Divac. Flagrant fouls : Barkley.

LA LAKERS	21	24	20	21	86
PHOENIX	24	19	27	11	81

Officials: Hugh Evans, Dan Crawford and Bob Delaney.
Attendance : 19,023.
Time: 2:23.

It's not over: With their team facing elimination in Game 3, Suns fans show their support in the Great Western Forum.

Phoenix's rookies gave the Suns CPR and prevented them from dying an ignominious playoff death.

Oliver Miller scored 11 points (including two huge free throws), had two blocks, four assists, eight rebounds and two steals, and Richard Dumas had 18 points and two steals to lead the Suns to a 107-102 victory May 4. The series stood at 2-1 in favor of the Lakers.

Phoenix Coach Paul Westphal had taken some criticism for not playing his rookies enough in the first two games of the series.

"I just try to go with guys who've done for us all year and the guys who are doing it that night," he said. "Sometimes those two things are in conflict."

Miller was grateful for the opportunity to play.

"It is kind of odd to have young guys in there at that time," he said. "We made some stupid rookie mistakes, but we made up for them. We have to make him (Westphal) look good. We can't let him down."

This time, the joke was on the Lakers. Ahead 43-39 at halftime, the Suns heard a bad joke from Coach Paul Westphal in the locker room and exploded in the second half to take a 101-86 victory over Los Angeles on May 6. The victory tied the series at 2-2.

Charles Barkley led the assault with 28 points and 11 rebounds. Rookie Oliver Miller played tough for a second straight game, scoring 16 points and grabbing eight rebounds, but more important, he limited Laker center Vlade Divac to 7-of-20 shooting.

But Westphal was still worried.

"It's not like they haven't beaten us (at home)," he said. "If we don't play well, they could beat us again."

Suns fans didn't seem worried, though. A crowd of about 5,000 showed up at the airport at 1 a.m. to welcome the Suns back to Phoenix.

Westphal thought the airport party was premature.

"I don't want to be a jerk or anything," he said, "but we've got a job to do, and we haven't finished yet."

Maybe Paul Westphal is a prophet. After losing Game 2, he declared that the Suns would win the last three games of the playoff series. On May 9, the Suns proved him right.

Led by Oliver Miller's nine points, five rebounds and one blocked shot (and that was just in overtime), the Suns sent Los Angeles home for the summer with a 112-104 victory at America West Arena, winning the series 3-2.

The Lakers had a chance to win a historic upset. After being hooked up to an IV overnight at a hospital, Suns guard Dan Majerle sank an 18-footer with 13.6 seconds left to tie the score at 95. Laker guard Byron Scott's three-point attempt at the buzzer fell short, sending the game into overtime.

Westphal called the series gut-wrenching.

"I've seen this team fight all year, and I thought we still had a lot of fight in us," he said. "It certainly didn't come easily — but I never predicted that it would come easily."

SUNS 107, LAKERS 102

PHOENIX

	Mn	FG	FT	Rb	At	PF	St	Tr	Pt
Barkley f	43	9-23	8-9	11	5	2	3	1	27
Dumas f	30	8-17	2-2	4	2	3	2	3	18
West c	18	1-5	3-4	9	0	4	0	1	5
KJohnson g	37	5-11	7-8	1	5	1	0	5	17
Majerle g	39	4-8	0-2	5	5	2	4	2	10
Miller	31	4-4	3-4	8	4	5	2	3	11
Ceballos	17	3-5	0-0	5	0	0	0	1	6
Ainge	20	5-6	0-0	1	3	2	1	2	13
Chambers	5	0-1	0-2	1	0	1	0	0	0
Totals		39-80	23-31	45	24	20	12	18	107

LA LAKERS

	Mn	FG	FT	Rb	At	PF	St	Tr	Pt
Campbell f	33	8-17	1-1	9	1	5	1	4	17
Green f	44	5-9	4-6	17	3	4	2	4	14
Divac c	34	11-22	6-8	8	6	5	1	3	30
Scott g	36	2-4	2-2	0	0	2	2	1	6
Threatt g	39	5-17	3-4	1	10	3	4	2	15
Worthy	30	6-18	1-1	6	4	4	2	2	13
Smith	12	1-3	0-0	1	0	1	0	0	2
Christie	12	2-5	0-0	1	0	1	0	1	5
Totals		40-95	17-22	43	24	24	13	16	102

FG percentage: Phoenix .488, LA Lakers .421.
FT percentage: Phoenix .742, LA Lakers .773.
Three-point shots: Phoenix 6-12 (Ainge 3-4, Majerle 2-4, Barkley 1-4), LA Lakers 5-14 (Divac 2-4, Threatt 2-4, Christie 1-2, Scott 0-1, Worthy 0-1, Green 0-2). **Blocked shots:** Phoenix 6 (West 2, Miller 2, Barkley, Ceballos), LA Lakers 6 (Divac 4, Campbell, Green). **Technicals:** Ceballos, Worthy. **Flagrant foul:** K. Johnson.

PHOENIX	27	24	34	22	107
LA LAKERS	24	20	32	26	102

Officials: Jess Kersey, Bernie Fryer and Bill Oakes.
Attendance: 17,505.
Time: 2:28.

SUNS 101, LAKERS 86

PHOENIX

	Mn	FG	FT	Rb	At	PF	St	Tr	Pt
Barkley f	39	13-21	2-4	11	4	1	2	0	28
Dumas f	23	4-11	6-8	6	3	3	1	0	14
West c	19	2-2	0-0	8	1	2	0	0	4
KJohnson g	39	7-16	2-3	4	6	3	0	3	16
Majerle g	43	3-10	0-0	5	3	3	0	2	8
Miller	29	7-11	2-5	8	2	2	1	2	16
Ceballos	5	0-1	0-0	1	1	1	0	0	0
Ainge	28	4-7	3-4	3	2	3	0	1	13
Chambers	12	1-3	0-0	3	0	2	1	0	2
FJohnson	3	0-0	0-0	0	0	1	0	0	0
Totals		41-82	15-24	49	22	21	5	8	101

LA LAKERS

	Mn	FG	FT	Rb	At	PF	St	Tr	Pt
Campbell f	30	4-11	4-10	7	0	4	0	2	12
Green f	45	2-6	1-2	15	1	0	1	3	5
Divac c	41	7-20	2-3	12	4	4	2	0	17
Scott g	34	3-9	4-4	3	4	1	0	2	10
Threatt g	37	6-14	1-1	3	6	3	0	3	13
Worthy	24	6-16	0-0	3	1	0	1	1	12
Christie	11	0-2	0-0	2	4	3	0	1	0
Smith	17	5-9	4-5	2	1	5	1	0	15
Cooper	1	0-3	0-0	2	1	0	0	0	0
Totals		33-90	16-25	49	22	20	5	12	86

FG percentage: Phoenix .500, LA Lakers .367.
FT percentage: Phoenix .625, LA Lakers .640.
Three-point shots: Phoenix 4-11 (Ainge 2-3, Barkley 0-2, Majerle 2-6), LA Lakers 4-14 (Scott 2-2, Smith 1-2, Divac 1-4, Green 0-1, Cooper, 0-1, Worthy 0-1, Christie 0-1, Threatt 0-2). **Blocked shots:** Phoenix 9 (Barkley 3, Dumas 2, West 2, Miller 2), LA Lakers 5 (Divac 3, Green, Threatt). **Technicals:** Chambers, Miller, K. Johnson, Barkley, Scott. **Flagrant foul:** Threatt.

PHOENIX	21	22	28	30	101
LA LAKERS	19	20	20	27	86

Officials: Jake O'Donnell, Jack Madden and Jim Clark.
Attendance: 17,505.
Time: 2:22.

SUNS 112, LAKERS 104

LA LAKERS

	Mn	FG	FT	Rb	At	PF	St	Tr	Pt
Campbell f	42	7-16	3-5	9	1	1	3	1	17
Green f	50	6-16	3-5	19	3	6	1	0	15
Divac c	21	6-8	0-0	4	6	5	0	2	12
Scott g	42	3-8	3-4	5	1	3	1	0	11
Threatt g	46	7-20	4-5	4	9	6	3	2	18
Edwards	6	1-2	0-0	0	0	0	0	0	2
Worthy	39	11-23	1-2	1	2	2	2	2	24
Smith	13	2-5	0-0	1	0	3	0	1	5
Christie	3	0-0	0-0	0	1	0	0	0	0
Cooper	3	0-3	0-0	0	0	0	0	0	0
Totals		43-101	14-21	43	23	26	10	8	104

PHOENIX

	Mn	FG	FT	Rb	At	PF	St	Tr	Pt
Barkley f	46	9-23	12-14	14	5	1	1	2	31
Dumas f	15	2-5	0-0	6	2	2	0	1	4
West c	13	1-1	0-0	3	1	0	0	0	2
KJohnson g	47	10-16	4-6	3	13	5	4	4	24
Majerle g	46	8-13	0-0	3	1	3	1	3	19
Miller	35	7-11	3-5	14	2	3	0	1	17
Ainge	37	2-6	4-4	7	3	2	0	2	9
Chambers	7	2-5	0-0	1	0	1	0	1	4
Ceballos	15	1-5	0-2	3	0	1	1	0	2
FJohnson	3	0-1	0-0	1	0	1	0	0	0
Knight g	1	0-0	0-0	0	0	0	0	0	0
Totals		42-86	23-31	55	27	18	7	14	112

FG percentage: LA Lakers .426, Phoenix .488.
FT percentage: LA Lakers .667, Phoenix .742.
Three-point shots: LA Lakers 4-15 (Scott 2-5, Worthy 1-2, Smith 1-2, Green 0-2, Threatt 0-2, Cooper 0-1), Phoenix 5-10 (Majerlie 3-7, Barkley 1-1, Ainge 1-2). **Blocked shots:** LA Lakers 7 (Campbell 5, Green, Divac), Phoenix 13 (Miller 7, Barkley, 2, Majerle 2, K. Johnson, Chambers). **Technicals:** K. Johnson.

LA LAKERS	24	21	26	24	9	104
PHOENIX	24	22	32	17	17	112

Officials: Dick Bavetta, Joe Crawford and Bennett Salvatore.
Attendance: 19,023.
Time: 2:48.

Charles Barkley
puts up a shot over
Vlade Divac during
Game 3.

Barkley celebrates
after scoring during
Game 4 in Los
Angeles.

Danny Ainge plays
mind games with
Divac in Game 5.

In Game 3, Kevin Johnson was able to control the ball against the Lakers' Sedale Threatt.

As time runs out in Game 4, the Suns' bench knows the series will return to Phoenix.

After Game 5, Oliver Miller joins his mentor on television.

ROUND 2: SPURS

Charles Barkley fights for a loose ball over the Spurs' Lloyd Daniels.

GAME 1 Kevin Johnson welcomed the Admiral and his fleet from San Antonio with 25 points, seven assists and five steals as the Suns won the opener of the Western Conference semifinals 98-89 on May 11.

The Suns grabbed a 1-0 lead in the best-of-seven series despite "Admiral" David Robinson's 32 points, 10 rebounds and seven blocked shots.

Suns rookie Richard Dumas, who played for Spurs Coach John Lucas on the Miami Tropics, a U.S. Basketball League team filled with players recovering from drug and alcohol addictions, scored 22 points.

KJ's performance prompted the Suns' point guard to speak out on his own behalf. "To be honest, I don't think there is a point guard in the league better than me," he said. "Before, there was Magic (Johnson). And in the last couple of years, there was (John) Stockton, (Mark) Price, (Tim) Hardaway and those guys.

"I'm a much more complete player than I've been in the past."

SUNS 98, SPURS 89

SAN ANTONIO

	Mn	FG	FT	Rb	At	PF	St	Tr	Pt
Carr f	33	9-14	1-3	8	5	6	1	1	19
Elliott f	40	3-13	2-2	1	3	2	1	2	8
Robinson c	43	13-20	6-10	10	4	4	3	4	32
Ellis g	24	1-4	0-1	3	2	0	1	1	2
A.Johnson g	16	2-5	0-0	3	1	2	0	3	4
Reid	13	0-3	2-4	5	1	1	0	0	2
Anderson	11	1-4	1-2	2	4	1	0	4	3
Del Negro	31	3-9	1-1	6	6	4	0	2	7
Daniels	22	4-10	0-0	9	1	0	2	1	8
Cummings	7	2-3	0-0	1	0	0	0	0	4
Totals		**38-85**	**13-23**	**48**	**27**	**20**	**8**	**18**	**89**

PHOENIX

	Mn	FG	FT	Rb	At	PF	St	Tr	Pt
Barkley f	39	5-21	8-9	10	3	2	2	3	18
Dumas f	38	9-12	4-4	3	2	1	2	2	22
West c	28	4-5	2-2	6	1	5	1	3	10
K.Johnson g	42	9-18	7-8	2	7	1	5	2	25
Majerle g	44	5-11	0-0	5	4	0	3	1	13
Miller	21	2-2	0-0	7	4	4	1	1	4
Ainge	12	2-7	2-2	2	2	2	1	1	6
Ceballos	5	0-0	0-0	1	0	0	0	0	0
Chambers	8	0-4	0-0	0	1	1	0	0	0
F.Johnson	3	0-0	0-0	0	0	0	0	0	0
Totals		**36-80**	**23-25**	**36**	**24**	**16**	**15**	**13**	**98**

FG percentage: San Antonio .447, Phoenix .450.
FT percentage: San Antonio .565, Phoenix .920.
Three-point shots: San Antonio 0-7 (Robinson 0-1, Ellis 0-1, Reid 0-1, Elliott 0-2, Daniels 0-2), Phoenix 3-10 (Majerle 3-4, Barkley 0-2, Ainge 0-4). **Blocked shots:** San Antonio 10 (Robinson 7, Carr, Anderson, Del Negro), Phoenix 12 (Miller 5, Dumas 2, Barkley, West, K. Johnson, Majerle, Ainge).
Technicals: Phoenix illegal defense,
K.Johnson. **Fouled out:** Carr.

SAN ANTONIO	19	19	28	23	89
PHOENIX	32	14	29	23	98

Officials: Darell Garretson, Lee Jones and Joe Forte.
Attendance: 19,023.
Time: 2:21.

Charles Barkley broke out of a brief slump with 35 points in Game 2.

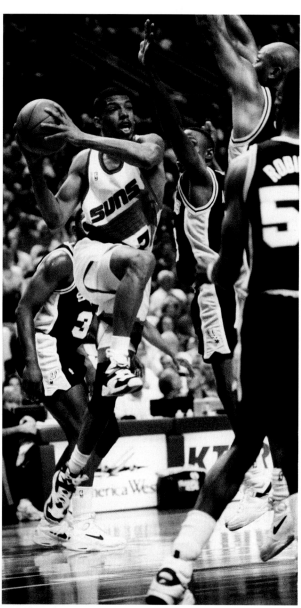

A slew of Spurs converges on KJ during Game 2.

Barkley and Danny Ainge know there is more work to do after losing Game 3 in San Antonio.

GAME 2

The 19,023 fans at America West Arena chanted "MVP, MVP" as Charles Barkley stepped up to the free-throw line with 3:31 left in the game May 13.

Although the fans were about two weeks earlier than the NBA in their MVP declaration, Barkley treated the throng to 35 points, 10 rebounds and a Suns playoff-record seven steals to lead the team to a 109-104 victory over the Spurs to take a 2-0 series lead.

Barkley's heroics came after two games in which Sir Charles had less than Barkley-like numbers.

"I just wanted to not hesitate," Barkley said.

"The last game, I started thinking too much."

The Suns squandered a 16-point fourth-quarter lead, and the Spurs were only four points down with about three minutes to play.

"We were not bright in the fourth quarter with our shot selection," Suns Coach Paul Westphal said.

GAME 3

The Suns traveled to the Alamo City only to be ambushed by a former University of Arizona star.

"Thing will be different today," Sean Elliott predicted before the game. He was right.

Elliott had 17 points, seven rebounds and four assists to help San Antonio defeat the Suns 111-96 on May 15 to cut the Suns' lead in the semifinals to 2-1.

The Suns helped the Spurs' effort by shooting a series-low 41 percent, with Dan Majerle making only two of 10 shots and seven Suns bench players shooting seven for 27.

"I'm not frustrated," Majerle insisted. Danny Ainge felt otherwise.

"I'm really frustrated," he said.

"The Spurs did what they said they were going to do," Phoenix Coach Paul Westphal said. "They came out aggressive, they got a lot more guys involved in their offense, and they basically just took the game."

GAME 4

The San Antonio Spurs called the Phoenix players "arrogant" after sending in the Admiral to sink the Suns.

In part, the Spurs were angry at pregame comments by Suns guard Kevin Johnson that they interpreted as guaranteeing victory.

David Robinson, their 7-foot-1 supercenter, scored 36 points, grabbed 16 rebounds and blocked three shots in a 117-103 defeat of the Suns on May 16 in the HemisFair Arena. The Spurs sent the Suns back to Phoenix with the series tied 2-2.

"You've got to give the Admiral credit," KJ said. "He was such a presence everywhere on the court."

The Spurs limited the Suns' superstar, Charles Barkley, to 18 points on 7-of-20 shooting despite losing starting forward Antoine Carr to a sprained left ankle in the first quarter.

KJ led the Suns with 26 points. Danny Ainge had 15, including nine on three-pointers.

SUNS 109, SPURS 103

SAN ANTONIO

	Mn	FG	FT	Rb	At	PF	St	Tr	Pt
Carr f	29	5-12	0-0	9	2	2	1	0	10
Elliott f	38	4-9	6-6	3	6	2	1	3	14
Robinson c	44	11-22	5-6	10	3	4	2	2	27
Ellis g	25	3-10	2-2	4	1	3	0	0	8
AJohnson g	25	5-6	0-1	5	6	5	2	5	10
Cummings	11	0-3	1-2	4	1	2	0	1	1
Anderson	14	0-5	0-0	0	1	2	0	0	0
Reid	20	2-3	4-4	3	0	4	0	1	8
Daniels	5	0-1	2-2	0	0	2	0	0	2
Del Negro	17	8-12	1-1	3	6	1	0	0	19
Smith	7	1-2	2-2	2	0	3	1	0	4
Wood	5	0-1	0-0	1	0	1	0	0	0
Totals		**39-86**	**23-26**	**44**	**26**	**31**	**7**	**12**	**103**

PHOENIX

	Mn	FG	FT	Rb	At	PF	St	Tr	Pt
Barkley f	35	12-18	10-14	10	2	2	7	0	35
Dumas f	31	5-9	2-3	4	3	3	0	2	12
West c	18	1-1	2-4	0	0	2	0	0	4
KJohnson g	34	3-7	9-10	2	12	2	0	2	15
Majerle g	48	7-16	3-7	1	4	3	0	1	18
Chambers	20	3-6	3-3	5	0	5	0	2	9
Ceballos	7	2-2	1-2	1	0	1	0	0	5
FJohnson	1	0-0	0-0	0	1	1	0	0	0
Ainge	20	1-7	0-1	6	1	3	0	2	3
Miller	26	4-4	0-0	3	4	3	0	0	8
Totals		**38-70**	**30-44**	**32**	**27**	**25**	**7**	**9**	**109**

FG percentage: San Antonio .453, Phoenix .543.
FT percentage: San Antonio .885, Phoenix .682.
Three-point shots: San Antonio 2-10 (Del Negro 2-4, A. Johnson 0-1, Daniels 0-1, Cummings 0-1, Ellis 0-3), Phoenix 3-10 (Ainge 1-3, Barkley 1-2, Majerle 1-5). **Blocked shots:** San Antonio 4 (Robinson 2, Elliott, Reid), Phoenix 12 (Miller 4, Barkley 3, West 3, K. Johnson 2). **Technical:** San Antonio Coach Lucas.

SAN ANTONIO	18	23	24	38	103
PHOENIX	25	27	26	31	109

Officials: Ed T. Rush, Hue Hollins and Bob Delaney.
Attendance: 19,023.
Time: 2:31.

SPURS 111, SUNS 96

PHOENIX

	Mn	FG	FT	Rb	At	PF	St	Tr	Pt
Dumas f	25	6-9	2-2	2	0	4	2	1	14
Barkley f	40	9-21	4-6	14	4	5	0	1	22
West c	11	2-2	1-1	1	0	1	0	0	5
KJohnson g	38	9-17	8-10	6	7	0	0	4	26
Majerle g	42	2-10	6-7	6	2	2	2	0	10
Chambers	16	1-7	1-2	4	0	1	0	1	3
Ceballos	11	4-9	0-0	4	0	0	0	0	8
Ainge	26	0-5	2-2	2	2	0	2	2	2
Miller	22	1-3	2-2	6	3	5	0	6	4
Mustaf	3	1-2	0-0	1	0	0	0	0	2
FJohnson	3	0-1	0-0	0	0	0	0	0	0
Knight	3	0-0	0-0	0	0	0	0	0	0
Totals		**35-86**	**26-32**	**44**	**18**	**20**	**4**	**15**	**96**

SAN ANTONIO

	Mn	FG	FT	Rb	At	PF	St	Tr	Pt
Elliott f	36	6-15	5-6	7	4	0	0	3	17
Carr f	29	10-14	1-2	6	0	3	1	1	21
Robinson c	28	4-16	5-7	8	6	4	1	2	13
Ellis g	39	9-16	2-2	6	0	4	0	0	20
AJohnson g	42	5-11	2-2	8	15	3	5	2	12
Del Negro	8	1-2	0-0	2	3	0	0	0	2
Smith	13	0-0	0-0	5	1	3	2	1	0
Reid	11	4-6	0-0	3	0	2	0	0	8
Cummings	13	6-11	0-0	6	0	3	1	0	12
Anderson	19	3-6	0-0	1	3	1	0	0	6
Wood	2	0-0	0-0	0	0	0	0	0	0
Totals		**48-97**	**15-19**	**52**	**32**	**23**	**10**	**9**	**111**

FG percentage: Phoenix .407, San Antonio .495.
FT percentage: Phoenix .813, San Antonio .789.
Three-point shots: Phoenix 0-10 (Dumas 0-1, Chambers 0-1, Majerle 0-2, Ainge 0-4); San Antonio 0-6 (Elliott 0-1, Del Negro 0-1, Anderson 0-1, Ellis 0-3). **Blocked shots:** Phoenix 7 (Miller 4, Barkley, K. Johnson, Mustaf); San Antonio 5 (Carr 2, Robinson, Johnson, Smith). **Technicals:** San Antonio illegal defense 3, Majerle, Miller.

PHOENIX	22	33	23	18	96
SAN ANTONIO	27	38	23	23	111

Officials: Mike.Mathis, Bill Oakes and Ron Garretson.
Attendance: 16,057.
Time: 2:16.

SPURS 117, SUNS 103

PHOENIX

	Mn	FG	FT	Rb	At	PF	St	Tr	Pt
Dumas f	30	3-11	1-1	2	2	3	1	3	7
Barkley f	41	7-20	4-6	12	4	5	0	6	18
West c	18	3-5	2-3	2	0	4	0	0	8
KJohnson g	43	7-14	12-14	2	8	2	1	1	26
Majerle g	44	6-16	2-4	5	3	3	0	1	16
Miller	27	1-3	2-4	9	3	5	2	0	4
Ainge	28	6-10	0-0	2	0	5	0	0	15
Chambers	6	1-4	3-4	2	1	2	0	0	5
Mustaf	1	1-1	0-0	0	0	0	0	0	2
FJohnson	1	0-0	2-2	0	0	0	0	0	2
Knight	1	0-1	0-0	0	0	0	0	0	0
Totals		**35-85**	**28-38**	**36**	**21**	**29**	**4**	**11**	**103**

SAN ANTONIO

	Mn	FG	FT	Rb	At	PF	St	Tr	Pt
Elliott f	37	7-13	5-6	5	2	3	0	3	19
Carr f	8	2-4	0-0	1	0	1	0	0	4
Robinson c	40	9-20	18-23	16	0	4	1	3	36
Ellis g	31	4-10	2-2	4	0	3	0	1	10
AJohnson g	37	2-7	2-2	3	12	4	0	2	6
Anderson	20	5-8	3-3	4	2	3	0	1	14
Reid	25	6-8	4-7	6	2	4	1	3	16
Del Negro	8	0-0	0-0	0	1	0	0	0	0
Cummings	13	3-8	0-0	7	1	4	0	0	6
Daniels	11	1-4	0-0	2	0	0	0	1	3
Smith	9	0-0	1-2	3	0	3	1	0	1
Wood	1	1-1	0-0	1	0	0	0	2	2
Totals		**40-83**	**35-45**	**52**	**20**	**29**	**3**	**14**	**117**

FG percentage: Phoenix .412, San Antonio .482.
FT percentage: Phoenix .737, San Antonio .778.
Three-point shots: Phoenix 5-17 (Ainge 3-5, Majerle 2-9, Barkley 0-2, K. Johnson 0-1); San Antonio 2-4 (Anderson 1-1, Daniels 1-1, Ellis 0-2). **Blocked shots:** Phoenix 5 (Miller 2, Majerle 2, Barkley); San Antonio 6 (Robinson 3, Carr 2, Elliott). **Technicals:** Phoenix illegal defense, Phoenix Coach Westphal. **Flagrant fouls:** Barkley.

PHOENIX	26	30	24	23	103
SAN ANTONIO	26	26	33	32	117

Officials: Jess Kersey, Jack Nies and Dan Crawford.
Attendance: 16,057.
Time: 2:32.

"I don't think there is a point guard in the league better than me," Kevin Johnson says after Game 1. He was frequently guarded by the much-taller Sean Elliott.

Charles Barkley, Richard Dumas and Oliver Miller suffered through a rough Game 4 in the Admiral's quarters.

GAME 5

Just as the Spurs relied on their superstar to lead them to victory in Game 4, the Suns watched their own superman break out of a scoring slump to score 19 points in the fourth quarter to push Phoenix to a 109-97 victory.

The Charles Barkley-led victory May 18 at America West Arena gave the Suns a 3-2 lead in the series.

The Spurs led after three quarters, but then Barkley took over the game, getting 19 of his game-high 36 points and six of his 12 rebounds.

"It didn't matter what they did, he was going to find a way to get the job done," Coach Paul Westphal said. "There have been guys who have risen to the occasion like him, but very few."

As the Suns were snatching the victory, John Lucas seemed more interested in towels. The Spurs coach was upset with towel-waving by Suns guard Negele Knight, which Lucas said interfered with Dale Ellis.

Lucas yelled his disapproval from several feet outside the coach's box.

Knight was undeterred.

"Coach Lucas doesn't understand what we're trying to say, and we don't understand what he's saying," Knight said. "It's no biggie."

SUNS 109, SPURS 97

SAN ANTONIO

	Mn	FG	FT	Rb	At	PF	St	Tr	Pt
Elliott f	43	6-15	3-3	5	8	1	1	2	15
Reid f	27	4-8	0-0	5	5	4	3	0	8
Robinson c	48	10-16	4-9	8	3	3	1	4	24
Ellis g	41	10-13	1-2	3	1	1	1	0	24
AJohnson g	46	6-10	0-0	2	15	4	1	4	12
Wood	8	1-1	0-0	1	1	3	0	0	3
Daniels	9	1-5	0-0	2	1	1	0	0	2
Anderson	7	3-6	0-0	1	1	1	0	0	7
Smith	6	0-0	0-0	0	0	3	0	0	0
Cummings	5	1-1	0-0	0	0	2	0	0	2
Totals		**42-75**	**8-14**	**27**	**35**	**23**	**7**	**10**	**97**

PHOENIX

	Mn	FG	FT	Rb	At	PF	St	Tr	Pt
Barkley f	44	11-16	13-15	12	3	4	0	3	36
Dumas f	15	4-6	2-2	1	1	1	0	1	10
West c	33	2-5	1-3	3	2	3	0	0	5
KJohnson g	38	7-9	1-2	6	12	1	0	3	15
Majerle g	43	8-17	1-1	4	2	1	0	1	17
Ceballos	14	4-4	0-0	1	3	2	0	0	8
FJohnson	11	2-2	2-2	1	1	0	0	0	6
Chambers	4	0-3	0-0	0	0	1	0	1	0
Miller	14	2-2	0-0	2	2	4	0	0	4
Ainge	24	3-8	0-0	1	2	2	1	1	8
Totals		**43-72**	**20-25**	**31**	**28**	**19**	**1**	**10**	**109**

FG percentage: San Antonio .560, Phoenix .597.
FT percentage: San Antonio .571, Phoenix .800.
Three-point shots: San Antonio 5-10 (Ellis 3-3, Wood 1-1, Anderson 1-1, Daniels 0-2, Elliott 0-3), Phoenix 3-8 (Ainge 2-4, Barkley 1-1, Majerle 0-3). **Blocked shots:** San Antonio 6 (Robinson 3, Reid 2, Elliott), Phoenix 8 (West 2, Majerle 2, Barkley, Dumas, Miller, K.Johnson).

SAN ANTONIO	29	31	23	14	97
PHOENIX	33	29	16	31	109

Officials: Hugh Evans, Bennett Salvatore and Don Vaden.
Attendance: 19,023.
Time: 2:13.

Forward Antoine Carr missed the rest of the series after spraining an ankle in Game 4.

Yes! Jerrod Mustaf hugs Frank Johnson after a Game 5 victory.

A dramatic Charles Barkley sprawls after being fouled on two of his 19 fourth-quarter points in Game 5.

KJ applies pressure to thwart his counterpart, Avery Johnson, in the series' final game.

Cedric Ceballos provides the drums for an unusual cheering technique used by Oliver Miller and Negele Knight as the Suns roll in Game 1.

GAME 6

It really didn't matter that Charles Barkley scored 28 points. It was his final two that sent San Antonio packing.

Barkley's 20-foot jumper with 1.8 seconds left gave the Suns a 102-100 victory over the Spurs on May 20 and moved the Suns into the Western Conference finals.

For good measure, Suns center Oliver Miller blocked a David Robinson desperation shot as time ran out.

"I knew David wasn't going to let me go to the basket," Barkley said. "So I kept driving him closer and closer. I knew it was in."

Robinson probably knew it, too.

"He hit it," the Admiral said. "That's why he's my choice for MVP."

The Suns, with a reputation for blowing big leads, actually were down by 10 points in the fourth quarter when they went on a 12-0 run to gain an 88-86 edge.

Forward Tom Chambers, star of Suns teams of the past, scored 10 points in 13 minutes on 5-of-9 shooting.

Guard Kevin Johnson scored 18, including seven successive points after the score was tied at 92 with 4:04 left.

SUNS 102, SPURS 100

PHOENIX

	Mn	FG	FT	Rb	At	PF	St	Tr	Pt
Dumas f	14	0-2	0-0	0	0	1	1	1	0
Barkley f	42	10-24	6-9	21	4	3	4	4	28
West c	15	1-2	0-0	3	0	1	0	1	2
KJohnson g	38	6-12	6-10	3	8	3	3	4	18
Majerle g	48	7-16	1-1	4	2	2	1	1	18
Ceballos	9	2-2	0-0	0	1	1	0	1	4
FJohnson	11	1-2	2-2	0	2	1	0	1	4
Ainge	25	2-8	1-2	1	4	4	0	0	6
Miller	25	5-8	2-4	5	1	4	2	1	12
Chambers	13	5-9	0-0	3	0	4	0	1	10
Totals		**39-85**	**18-28**	**40**	**22**	**23**	**11**	**14**	**102**

SAN ANTONIO

	Mn	FG	FT	Rb	At	PF	St	Tr	Pt
Reid f	30	6-14	2-2	2	1	4	0	3	14
Elliott f	36	8-14	2-2	11	0	1	0	2	19
Robinson c	42	6-15	10-14	14	5	2	2	2	22
Ellis g	27	4-11	0-0	1	0	3	0	2	11
AJohnson g	33	5-9	0-1	2	10	4	1	2	10
Anderson	34	4-8	3-4	4	2	5	2	2	13
Smith	4	0-0	0-0	0	0	0	0	0	0
Del Negro	13	1-4	0-0	4	4	4	1	0	2
Cummings	20	4-7	1-2	2	1	5	2	2	9
Daniels	1	0-0	0-0	0	0	0	0	0	0
Totals		**38-82**	**18-25**	**39**	**23**	**25**	**7**	**15**	**100**

FG Percentage: Phoenix .459, San Antonio .463.
FT percentage: Phoenix .643, San Antonio .720.
Three-point shots: Phoenix 6-12 (Majerle 3-5, Barkley 2-5, Ainge 1-2), San Antonio 6-13 (Ellis 3-6, Anderson 2-4, Robinson 1-3). **Blocked shots:** Phoenix 8 (Miller 5, Barkley 2, Majerle), San Antonio 8 (Robinson 4, Reid 2, Anderson, Smith).

PHOENIX	32	24	20	26	102
SAN ANTONIO	26	32	25	17	100

Officials: Jake O'Donnell, Jack Madden and Steve Javie.
Attendance: 16,057.
Time: 2:30.

ROUND 3: SONICS

GAME 1 Charles Barkley was officially named the NBA's Most Valuable Player before the May 24 opener of the Western Conference Finals, but another Suns forward took charge that day to lead Phoenix to a 105-91 victory over the Seattle SuperSonics.

Making only his second start of the playoffs, Cedric Ceballos scored 21 points in 23 minutes.

Oliver Miller had 15 points, 10 rebounds and five blocked shots.

"They thought I was still in Philly and I don't have help," Barkley said after his 12-point, 14-rebound performance. "I've been telling you (media) guys all year — we've got guys who can make plays."

Suns Coach Paul Westphal said he started Ceballos on a "whim."

Ceballos, however, jokingly disagreed: "I think Paul's dog decides. When Paul gets up in the morning, if his dog licks his left hand, he goes with Richard (Dumas). If his dog licks his right hand, he starts me."

Dan Majerle fights his way past Derrick McKey and Gary Payton.

Game-winner: A fadeaway jumper by Sir Charles (opposite page) over David Robinson.

Cedric Ceballos, the game's leading scorer, played only 23 minutes before aggravating a foot injury.

SUNS 105, SONICS 91

SEATTLE

	Mn	FG	FT	Rb	At	PF	St	Tr	Pt
Kemp f	39	6-11	4-4	10	5	5	1	4	16
McKey f	34	6-10	5-7	5	4	2	1	0	17
Perkins c	26	3-11	0-0	3	0	1	1	3	9
Payton g	33	6-11	2-4	4	3	5	2	4	14
Pierce g	18	3-8	0-0	1	0	4	0	2	6
McMillan	28	3-12	0-0	6	7	3	4	0	6
Cage	13	2-3	0-1	3	0	0	1	1	4
EJohnson	16	2-6	0-0	2	1	4	0	1	4
Askew	11	2-5	1-1	1	1	2	0	1	5
Paddio	5	1-2	0-0	0	1	0	0	0	2
Barros	14	1-6	0-0	3	1	0	0	1	2
Scheffler	3	1-2	4-4	2	0	1	0	0	6
Totals		**36-87**	**16-21**	**40**	**23**	**27**	**10**	**17**	**91**

PHOENIX

	Mn	FG	FT	Rb	At	PF	St	Tr	Pt
Barkley f	36	6-14	0-0	14	2	2	0	3	12
Ceballos f	23	8-12	5-6	3	3	1	0	1	21
West c	18	2-3	0-0	3	1	1	0	0	4
KJohnson g	32	7-10	2-3	3	6	2	3	2	16
Majerle g	45	4-10	0-0	5	9	3	2	3	9
Ainge	24	4-13	0-0	1	3	4	0	2	11
Chambers	15	1-5	1-1	3	1	2	1	0	3
FJohnson	16	3-5	2-3	2	2	1	0	0	8
Miller	25	5-7	5-10	10	4	3	2	4	15
Dumas	4	1-1	2-2	0	0	1	0	0	4
Knight	2	1-2	0-0	0	0	0	0	0	2
Totals		**42-82**	**17-25**	**44**	**31**	**20**	**8**	**15**	**105**

FG percentage: Seattle .414, Phoenix .512.
FT percentage: Seattle .762, Phoenix .680.
Three-point shots: Seattle 3-9 (Perkins 3-4, McMillan 0-1, E.Johnson 0-1, Barros 0-1, Pierce 0-2), Phoenix 4-13 (Ainge 3-7, Majerle 1-3, Barkley 0-3). **Blocked shots:** Seattle 9 (Perkins 4, Kemp 2, McMillan 2, McKey), Phoenix 16 (Miller 5, West 4, Ceballos 2, Chambers 2, Barkley, Majerle, Ainge).

SEATTLE	23	24	18	26	91
PHOENIX	24	27	25	29	105

Officials: Darell Garretson, Jess Kersey and Ed T.Rush.
Attendance: 19,023.
Time: 2:16.

Seattle's Ricky Pierce found his way to the hoop often in Game 2, leading all scorers with 34 points.

Charles Barkley took a little teasing after his MVP award was presented before Game 1.

GAME 2

The Suns proved there's nothing free about free throws.

Even though they were at home, the Suns missed 15 free throws, finished 26 for 41 at the charity line and lost to Seattle, 103-99 on May 26 at America West Arena.

SuperSonics guard Ricky Pierce was the high scorer, with 34 points, and Sonics center Sam Perkins hit two key three-pointers — one with 9.8 seconds left — to add to the Suns' misery.

The loss offset a career playoff high for Suns guard Dan Majerle, who scored 29 points, grabbed 10 rebounds and had four assists, three blocked shots and a steal.

"My scoring doesn't mean anything for this team," Majerle said. "The bottom line is wins and losses."

Phoenix Coach Paul Westphal was not happy with the statistics.

"We didn't have many turnovers (13), we shot a relatively decent percentage (48.6), but the main thing was the free throws," he said. "We could have had a nice cushion and they'd have had to play us differently."

GAME 3

When the Suns met the Sonics in Seattle on May 28, about 7,400 Phoenix fans coughed up $3 each for Suns' Charities to watch the game on big-screen TV at America West Arena.

They saw reserve guard Frank Johnson score 10 points in 13 minutes to spark the Suns to a 104-97 win and a 2-1 lead in the series.

"He's got a great heart," said Suns forward Cedric Ceballos. "He scratches. He claws. He does everything you ask him to."

Johnson was one of seven Suns scoring in double figures. Charles Barkley had 16 points (only two came in the second half, but they were a big two scored off a missed free throw with 1:50 remaining).

The win allowed the Suns to regain home-court advantage.

"To be honest, I think they (the Sonics) rely on their bench more than we rely on ours," said backup guard Danny Ainge, who scored seven points. "So if our bench can outscore their (bench), then it's a big advantage to us."

GAME 4

The Suns may have been defensive after their 120-101 loss to the SuperSonics in Seattle on May 30, but they sure weren't defensive during the game.

The bigger Sonics had their way with the Suns, evening the Western Conference Finals at two games apiece.

"They outrebounded us, forced turnovers, got us out of our offense, outhustled us. What else is there?" asked Suns Coach Paul Westphal.

"Coaching?" someone asked.

"Fine," Westphal answered.

Seattle's big men — Shawn Kemp, Derrick McKey and Sam Perkins — combined for 59 points and 21 rebounds.

The Suns were led by Charles Barkley, who had 27 points and seven rebounds. But Barkley scored only four points in the second half.

Dan Majerle, with 16 points, was the only other starter in double figures.

"This was the first time I've felt we quit all year long," said Suns guard Danny Ainge. "You saw what I saw. It just wasn't important enough to us."

SONICS 103, SUNS 99

SEATTLE

	Mn	FG	FT	Rb	At	PF	St	Tr	Pt
Kemp f	33	5-5	6-8	6	0	3	0	2	16
McKey f	24	1-7	1-2	3	2	4	0	1	3
Perkins c	33	5-18	6-6	7	2	4	1	1	19
Payton g	28	4-11	0-3	6	3	6	3	1	8
Pierce g	40	13-20	7-8	2	2	4	0	0	34
Cage	25	4-7	0-0	6	0	2	1	1	8
McMillan	18	0-4	0-0	8	6	3	1	3	0
EJohnson	18	2-7	3-3	2	0	2	0	0	7
Barros	15	1-3	2-2	0	2	0	0	1	4
Askew	4	2-2	0-0	1	0	0	0	0	4
Paddio	1	0-0	0-0	0	0	0	0	0	0
Scheffler	1	0-0	0-0	0	0	0	0	0	0
Totals		**37-84**	**25-32**	**41**	**17**	**28**	**6**	**10**	**103**

PHOENIX

	Mn	FG	FT	Rb	At	PF	St	Tr	Pt
Barkley f	44	9-19	6-8	10	6	3	0	0	24
Ceballos f	14	3-3	4-6	2	0	2	0	1	10
West c	9	0-1	0-0	1	0	2	0	2	0
KJohnson g	39	3-8	6-11	2	4	3	2	3	12
Majerle g	48	10-18	5-9	10	4	4	1	3	29
Dumas	9	2-3	2-2	1	0	2	0	1	6
Chambers	21	1-6	0-0	3	1	4	0	0	2
FJohnson	9	0-0	0-0	1	2	1	0	1	0
Ainge	16	1-6	3-3	1	3	1	1	0	6
Miller	31	5-6	0-2	8	2	3	2	2	10
Totals		**34-70**	**26-41**	**39**	**22**	**25**	**6**	**13**	**99**

FG percentage: Seattle .440, Phoenix .486.
FT percentage: Seattle .781, Phoenix .634.
Three-point shots: Seattle 4-11 (Perkins 3-7, Pierce 1-2, McMillan 0-1, Johnson 0-1), Phoenix 5-14 (Majerle 4-8, Ainge 1-4, Barkley 0-2). **Blocked shots:** Seattle 8 (Kemp 7, Cage), Phoenix 13 (Ceballos 3, Majerle 3, Miller 3, K.Johnson 2, West, Chambers). **Technicals:** Seattle Coach Karl, Seattle illegal defense, Ceballos.

SEATTLE	18	30	22	33	103
PHOENIX	24	30	22	23	99

Officials: Mike Mathis, B. Salvatore and Ronnie Nunn.
Attendance: 19,023.
Time: 2:31.

SUNS 104, SONICS 97

PHOENIX

	Mn	FG	FT	Rb	At	PF	St	Tr	Pt
Barkley f	42	7-20	2-3	16	2	4	4	2	16
Dumas f	18	5-8	1-2	1	0	2	1	2	11
West c	19	0-3	2-4	6	0	1	0	1	2
KJohnson g	35	5-7	10-14	1	9	4	0	2	20
Majerle g	34	3-8	3-4	6	3	4	1	0	10
Miller	18	1-2	2-4	2	1	3	1	0	4
Ceballos	18	5-11	4-4	4	0	0	3	0	14
Chambers	16	3-6	4-4	0	0	3	2	2	10
FJohnson	13	4-5	1-2	0	1	4	0	0	10
Ainge	27	3-6	0-0	2	4	2	1	0	7
Totals		**36-76**	**29-41**	**38**	**20**	**27**	**13**	**9**	**104**

SEATTLE

	Mn	FG	FT	Rb	At	PF	St	Tr	Pt
Kemp f	41	5-14	9-10	12	1	5	2	4	19
McKey f	40	6-14	6-8	11	3	5	4	2	18
Perkins c	34	5-13	2-2	10	2	5	1	0	13
Payton g	31	4-10	0-0	4	2	4	1	3	8
Pierce g	37	10-19	7-7	5	3	2	0	0	28
Cage	15	2-3	0-0	6	0	2	0	1	4
McMillan	23	2-6	2-4	4	5	3	0	4	6
EJohnson	14	0-6	0-0	3	0	1	0	4	0
Barros	5	0-0	1-2	0	0	2	0	0	1
Totals		**34-85**	**27-33**	**55**	**16**	**29**	**8**	**18**	**97**

FG percentage : Phoenix .474, Seattle .400.
FT percentage: Phoenix .707, Seattle .818.
Three-point shots: Phoenix 3-11 (F. Johnson 1-1, Majerle 1-4, Ainge 1-4, Barkley 0-2), Seattle 2-11 (Pierce 1-2, Perkins 1-6, McMillan 0-3). **Blocked shots:** Phoenix 6 (West 2, Miller 2, Barkley, K. Johnson), Seattle 7 (Kemp 3, Cage 2, Perkins, McMillan).

PHOENIX	32	25	23	24	104
SEATTLE	25	31	24	17	97

Officials: Ed Rush, Ron Garretson, Dick Bavetta.
Attendance: 14,812.
Time: 2:27.

SONICS 120, SUNS 101

PHOENIX

	Mn	FG	FT	Rb	At	PF	St	Tr	Pt
Barkley f	39	11-20	4-5	7	4	5	2	5	27
Dumas f	19	2-7	0-0	1	0	3	1	1	4
West c	13	2-4	0-0	5	1	3	1	0	4
KJohnson g	35	2-11	2-3	1	7	2	1	4	6
Majerle g	42	6-14	0-0	5	4	2	2	1	16
Miller	23	5-9	1-2	3	1	3	0	3	11
Ceballos	10	2-2	0-0	4	0	1	0	1	4
Ainge	26	2-4	3-3	3	3	4	1	0	9
Chambers	20	3-8	8-10	4	0	2	0	1	14
FJohnson	11	1-5	2-2	1	1	1	2	2	4
Knight	2	1-1	0-0	0	0	0	0	1	2
Totals		**37-85**	**20-25**	**34**	**21**	**26**	**10**	**19**	**101**

SEATTLE

	Mn	FG	FT	Rb	At	PF	St	Tr	Pt
Kemp f	33	8-13	4-5	8	3	6	2	5	20
McKey f	39	6-9	8-11	7	6	2	0	1	20
Perkins c	34	5-11	9-11	6	4	4	0	2	19
Payton g	24	5-10	0-0	3	5	3	1	3	10
Pierce g	25	3-7	2-2	3	2	2	0	2	8
McMillan	22	3-7	0-0	5	5	3	6	1	6
EJohnson	25	5-9	2-2	3	0	4	0	4	12
Cage	11	4-8	0-0	7	0	1	0	0	8
Barros	18	4-6	0-0	1	2	0	0	0	9
Askew	6	2-3	0-0	1	0	1	0	1	4
Paddio	2	1-1	0-0	1	0	0	0	0	2
Scheffler	1	1-3	0-0	2	0	0	0	0	2
Totals		**47-87**	**25-31**	**46**	**28**	**26**	**9**	**19**	**120**

FG percentage: Phoenix .435, Seattle .540.
FT percentage: Phoenix .800, Seattle .806.
Three-point shots: Phoenix 7-19 (Majerle 4-9, Ainge 2-3, Barkley 1-5, F.Johnson 0-1, Chambers 0-1), Seattle 1-7 (Barros 1-2, Perkins 0-3, Pierce 0-1, E.Johnson 0-1). **Blocked shots:** Phoenix 3 (West 2, Barkley), Seattle 8 (Kemp 4, Perkins 2, McKey, Askew). **Technicals:** Barkley, K. Johnson, E. Johnson, Phoenix illegal defense, Seattle illegal defense. **Fouled out:** Kemp.

PHOENIX	29	29	18	25	101
SEATTLE	37	24	26	33	120

Officials: Jake O'Donnell, Hue Hollins and Dan Crawford.
Attendance: 14,812.
Time: 2:32.

Sam Perkins asks for a timeout after Danny Ainge, assisted by Oliver Miller, leaves him no place to go in Game 7.

Charles Barkley draws a crowd as he moves to the hoop in Game 7.

Kevin Johnson battles Seattle's Nate McMillan for a loose ball in Game 2.

Dan Majerle finds himself in the path of an angry Michael Cage as referee Darell Garretson moves in to break up a Game 6 scuffle.

Ex-Sun Eddie Johnson doesn't have the height to defend against Tom Chambers in Game 5.

Charles Barkley carried on a lively debate with Seattle fans in Game 4, much of it unprintable.

Who, me? Danny Ainge disputes a Game 4 foul call.

Seattle fans taunt Barkley, although he pretends not to hear.

Barkley, hit with a technical as the Suns struggled in Game 6, pleads his case to no avail.

Dan Majerle happily acknowledges fans after hitting eight three-pointers in Game 5, a playoff record.

GAME 5

For Charles Barkley it was a triple double. For Dan Majerle, it was just a triple — eight times.

Barkley, who cursed at teammates in Game 4 and demanded that they get him the ball more often, scored 43 points, had 15 rebounds and 10 assists to lead the Suns to a 120-114 victory on June 1.

Majerle eclipsed his Game 2 career playoff high with 34 points, with the help of an NBA playoff record eight three-pointers.

Together they helped give the Suns a 3-2 lead over Seattle.

"I just demanded the ball," Barkley said after the game. "I hadn't been getting it in the second half the whole series. Sometimes, we try to get others involved instead of getting me involved."

The Sonics did not go quietly, however.

Forward Shawn Kemp scored 26 of his 33 points in the second half, and the Sonics were only one point down with about 20 seconds left when Majerle sealed the win with his eighth three.

GAME 6

It was too much to hope for Dan Majerle and Charles Barkley to repeat their game-winning heroics of Game 5. In fact, the Suns had very few heroes in their 118-102 loss in Seattle.

The loss June 3 tied the series 3-3, sending both teams back to Phoenix for the deciding game.

The Sonics limited Barkley to 13 points and Majerle to 12, while Seattle guard Ricky Pierce scored 27 and Shawn Kemp 22. The Sonics were also more physical, resulting in two minor scuffles: the first between Suns guard Danny Ainge and Sonics forward Michael Cage, and the second between Suns guard Frank Johnson and Pierce.

"Our execution wasn't very good," Ainge said. "And it seemed like every time we turned it over, they scored on the fast break. That kills you."

To add injury to insult, Suns forward Cedric Ceballos came off the bench to score eight quick points, only to break a bone in his left foot after four minutes. The injury, which required surgery, kept Ceballos out of Game 7 and the NBA Finals.

GAME 7

Charles Barkley had the starring role.

He scored 44 points and grabbed 24 rebounds as the Suns scorched Seattle 123-110 on June 5. The march to the NBA Finals was complete.

Sir Charles had a strong supporting cast — Kevin Johnson, 22 points and 9 assists; Mark West, 11 points (nine in the first quarter); and Tom Chambers, starting for the first time this season, 17 points and six rebounds.

"I'm glad (Coach) Paul (Westphal) gave me the opportunity to show what I could do, and had confidence in me," Chambers said.

The Suns, helpless from the free-throw line in Game 2, made 57 of 64 free-throw attempts, tying a playoff record.

The SuperSonics rallied in the second half behind Eddie Johnson's 34 points, but Seattle was doomed.

In a postgame tirade against the media for their lack of respect for the Suns, Barkley summed up the hard-fought Sonics series: "Call us whatever you want, but call us Western Conference champions."

SUNS 120, SONICS 114

SEATTLE

	Mn	FG	FT	Rb	At	PF	St	Tr	Pt
Kemp f	32	13-18	7-9	6	4	4	1	3	33
McKey f	38	3-6	3-4	4	5	4	2	1	9
Perkins c	38	3-10	4-5	6	5	4	4	1	10
Payton g	38	10-18	0-0	2	8	2	3	0	20
Pierce g	32	9-17	6-7	1	5	1	1	1	27
Cage	23	2-2	1-2	2	1	3	1	2	5
EJohnson	15	3-7	0-0	2	0	2	0	0	7
McMillan	19	1-3	1-2	2	7	4	1	1	3
Barros	5	0-1	0-0	0	0	2	1	1	0
Totals		44-82	22-29	25	35	26	14	10	114

PHOENIX

	Mn	FG	FT	Rb	At	PF	St	Tr	Pt
Barkley f	47	16-22	11-11	15	10	2	2	3	43
Dumas f	17	1-5	2-4	1	0	4	0	1	4
West c	25	0-1	1-2	5	0	6	1	1	1
KJohnson g	36	5-11	3-4	2	10	1	2	5	13
Majerle g	47	12-17	2-2	7	4	3	1	2	34
Ceballos	3	0-1	0-0	0	1	1	0	0	0
Ainge	11	0-1	2-2	1	1	1	0	0	2
FJohnson	13	1-2	2-2	2	0	3	0	1	4
Miller	22	4-7	0-0	5	5	2	2	4	8
Chambers	17	5-14	0-0	4	1	3	0	0	11
Mustaf	1	0-0	0-0	0	0	0	0	0	0
Knight	0	0-0	0-0	0	0	0	0	0	0
Totals		44-81	23-27	42	32	26	8	17	120

FG percentage: Seattle .537, Phoenix .543.
FT percentage: Seattle .759, Phoenix .852.
Three-point shots: Seattle 4-7 (Pierce 3-3, E. Johnson 1-1, Perkins 0-1, Barros 0-1, McMillan 0-1), Phoenix 9-12 (Majerle 8-10, Chambers 1-1, Ainge 0-1). Blocked shots: Seattle 11 (McKey 5, Kemp 3, Perkins, Pierce, McMillan), Phoenix 8 (West 3, Barkley 2, Majerle, Ceballos, Miller). Fouled out: West.

SEATTLE	28	26	27	33	114
PHOENIX	28	31	25	36	120

Officials: Jack Madden, Joe Crawford and Steve Javie.
Attendance: 19,023.
Time: 2:26.

SONICS 118, SUNS 102

PHOENIX

	Mn	FG	FT	Rb	At	PF	St	Tr	Pt
Barkley f	38	4-14	5-8	11	3	3	1	3	13
Dumas f	11	1-4	0-0	3	0	1	1	1	2
West c	13	1-3	0-0	5	0	4	0	1	2
KJohnson g	38	8-15	6-7	3	4	2	0	5	22
Majerle g	44	4-11	3-4	7	3	3	1	1	12
Chambers	16	4-6	0-0	2	0	3	0	2	8
FJohnson	14	2-4	4-6	1	2	3	1	0	8
Miller	27	6-12	2-3	6	2	2	2	1	14
Ainge	31	2-10	2-2	2	2	4	0	1	7
Ceballos	4	3-4	2-2	1	0	0	0	0	8
Mustaf	2	1-2	0-0	1	0	0	0	0	2
Knight	2	2-3	0-0	0	1	0	0	0	4
Totals		38-88	24-32	42	17	25	6	15	102

SEATTLE

	Mn	FG	FT	Rb	At	PF	St	Tr	Pt
Kemp f	37	8-12	6-8	15	4	5	1	2	22
McKey f	36	8-12	0-0	3	5	3	1	1	16
Perkins c	35	6-12	2-2	5	2	4	3	0	18
Payton g	29	6-15	4-6	5	4	4	1	1	16
Pierce g	33	9-15	8-8	4	2	2	3	2	27
EJohnson	19	1-6	4-4	3	0	2	1	1	6
McMillan	20	2-6	1-2	3	4	6	1	5	5
Cage	20	3-4	0-0	10	2	2	1	2	6
Barros	7	0-3	0-0	1	1	1	0	0	0
Paddio	2	1-1	0-0	1	1	0	0	0	2
Scheffler	2	0-2	0-0	0	0	0	0	0	0
Totals		44-88	25-30	50	25	29	12	14	118

FG percentage: Phoenix .432, Seattle .500.
FT percentage: Phoenix .750, Seattle .833.
Three-point shots: Phoenix 2-15 (Majerle 1-4, Ainge 1-6, Barkley 0-3, F. Johnson 0-1, Miller 0-1), Seattle 5-14 (Perkins 4-9, Pierce 1-2, E. Johnson 0-1, McMillan 0-1, Barros 0-1). Blocked shots: Phoenix 4 (Barkley, Knight, West, Miller), Seattle 10 (Kemp 3, Perkins 3, McMillan 2, McKey, Pierce). Technicals: Barkley, Ainge, Cage, Seattle illegal defense 2.

PHOENIX	25	25	25	27	102
SEATTLE	27	34	25	32	118

Officials: Bill Oakes, Hugh Evans and Darell Garretson.
Attendance: 14,812.
Time: 2:33.

SUNS 123, SONICS 110

SEATTLE

	Mn	FG	FT	Rb	At	PF	St	Tr	Pt
Kemp f	39	5-12	8-10	8	3	6	2	4	18
McKey f	31	3-7	0-0	3	5	3	0	3	6
Perkins c	31	7-13	3-3	3	1	2	0	0	19
Payton g	29	3-7	3-5	2	3	4	1	1	9
Pierce g	24	2-8	3-4	2	3	5	0	2	7
EJohnson	26	12-17	9-9	2	0	6	0	2	34
McMillan	23	3-8	2-4	1	7	6	1	1	9
Cage	9	0-1	0-0	6	0	2	0	0	0
Askew	16	3-3	0-1	3	3	4	0	1	6
Barros	8	1-2	0-0	1	1	0	0	0	2
Paddio	3	0-0	0-0	0	0	1	0	0	0
Scheffler	1	0-0	0-0	0	0	0	1	0	0
Totals		39-78	28-36	31	26	38	5	14	110

PHOENIX

	Mn	FG	FT	Rb	At	PF	St	Tr	Pt
Barkley f	46	12-20	19-22	24	1	3	1	1	44
Chambers f	29	5-13	6-6	6	1	4	0	0	17
West c	24	3-5	5-6	2	0	3	1	1	11
KJohnson g	39	4-11	14-16	2	9	4	4	4	22
Majerle g	45	3-11	4-4	7	7	2	2	1	11
Ainge	27	3-6	4-4	4	3	5	2	0	13
Miller	16	0-2	1-2	1	0	3	0	2	1
FJohnson	12	0-4	4-4	0	0	3	0	0	4
Mustaf	1	0-0	0-0	0	0	0	0	0	0
Knight	1	0-0	0-0	0	0	0	0	0	0
Totals		30-72	57-64	46	21	27	10	10	123

FG percentage: Seattle .500, Phoenix .417.
FT percentage: Seattle .778, Phoenix .891.
Three-point shots: Seattle 4-10 (Perkins 2-5, E. Johnson 1-1, McMillan 1-2, Pierce 0-1, Barros 0-1), Phoenix 6-12 (Ainge 3-5, Barkley 1-1, Chambers 1-2, Majerle 1-4). Blocked shots: Seattle 7 (Kemp 2, McKey 2, Perkins 2, Cage), Phoenix 11 (Chambers 2, West 2, K.Johnson 2, Majerle 2, Miller 2, Barkley). Technicals: Miller, Payton, Ainge. Fouled out: Kemp, E. Johnson, McMillan.

SEATTLE	26	25	29	30	110
PHOENIX	31	26	34	32	123

Officials: Ed T. Rush, Dick Bavetta and Mike Mathis.
Attendance: 19,023.
Time: 2:42.

Unhappy with Game 5 officiating, Sir Charles takes aim.

Dan Majerle scored 24 of his 34 points in Game 5 from afar, which opened up some driving room.

Cedric Ceballos' last minutes on the court are filled with pain. He would not return after Game 6.

Fouls are painful to Charles Barkley, who protests a call in Game 7.

For veterans Charles Barkley and Tom Chambers, the trip to the championship series was a long time coming.

Frank Johnson savors the win and its rewards.

On to the finals: Everyone you meet seems to be a Suns fan these days.

As pandemonium sweeps America West Arena after Game 7, Charles Barkley spends a moment with Sonics Coach George Karl.

THE FINALS

The Suns saved Chicago from itself.
Down 3-1 as they went into the fifth game, the Suns were
given no chance and no respect by Bulls fans. Champagne
was chilling. Storefronts were boarded up, extra police
were on the street, and the forecast was a riot-and-revel
celebration of Chicago's third successive NBA title.
The Suns kept the peace by winning the battle and
bringing the series home to America West Arena.

GAME 1 Maybe it was nerves.

Eighteen minutes into the Suns' biggest game in 17 years, they found themselves down 20 points to the two-time NBA champion Chicago Bulls on June 9.

"We acted like it was just good to be here instead of playing to win," Suns assistant Scotty Robertson said.

Charles Barkley and Kevin Johnson, who brought the team to the NBA Finals, struggled. Barkley had 21 points, but was nine for 25 from the field. Johnson had 11 points, with more turnovers (five) than assists (two).

The Suns fought back gamely, bringing the score to 88-85 with 4:26 to play before the Bulls pulled away.

One bright spot was Richard Dumas, who broke out of a playoff slump with 20 points, 12 rebounds, four assists and two steals.

As they have all year, Michael Jordan, with 31 points, and Scottie Pippen, with 27, led the Bulls. B.J. Armstrong added 16, plus tenacious defense against KJ.

Just the bigness of the event was overwhelming — 109 countries watching, and the biggest media horde this side of the White House.

"We got off to a bad start — whatever you want to call it, nerves," Barkley said.

"Our experience in the playoffs probably won us this game," Bulls Coach Phil Jackson said.

BULLS 100, SUNS 92

CHICAGO

	Mn	FG	FT	Rb	At	PF	St	Tr	Pt
Grant f	44	5-9	1-1	7	5	2	0	1	11
Pippen f	39	12-20	3-9	9	5	3	2	3	27
Cartwright c	25	4-5	1-2	3	3	3	2	1	9
Armstrong g	38	5-9	3-3	3	5	3	1	0	16
Jordan g	43	14-28	3-4	7	5	2	5	2	31
Williams	23	2-5	0-0	10	2	2	0	3	4
Paxson	16	1-3	0-0	1	3	2	0	0	2
Tucker	9	0-1	0-0	0	0	0	0	2	0
King	3	0-1	0-0	1	0	0	0	0	0
Totals		**43-81**	**11-19**	**41**	**28**	**17**	**10**	**12**	**100**

PHOENIX

	Mn	FG	FT	Rb	At	PF	St	Tr	Pt
Barkley f	46	9-25	2-3	11	5	4	1	2	21
Dumas f	42	10-20	0-0	12	4	4	2	1	20
West c	14	3-3	0-1	2	0	2	0	1	6
KJohnson g	36	4-13	3-3	2	2	0	1	5	11
Majerle g	43	6-11	3-3	8	2	2	1	3	16
Miller	27	2-5	2-4	5	3	4	1	0	6
Chambers	3	0-2	0-0	0	0	0	0	1	0
Ainge	20	2-4	0-1	1	1	3	0	0	4
FJohnson	9	4-7	0-0	1	1	0	0	0	8
Totals		**40-90**	**10-15**	**42**	**18**	**19**	**6**	**13**	**92**

FG percentage: Chicago .531, Phoenix .444
FT percentage: Chicago .579, Phoenix .667
Three-point shots: Chicago 3-8 (Armstrong 3-4, Jordan 0-1, Paxson 0-1, Pippen 0-2), Phoenix 2-7 (Barkley 1-1, Majerle 1-4, K. Johnson 0-1, Ainge 0-1). **Blocked shot:** Chicago 8 (S. Williams 3, Grant 2, Cartwright, Jordan, Paxson), Phoenix 10 (Majerle 4, Dumas 3, Miller 3). **Technicals:** Paxson, Chicago illegal defense 2, Phoenix illegal defense.

CHICAGO	34	18	21	27	100
PHOENIX	20	21	28	23	92

Officials: Hugh Evans, Jess Kersey and Hue Hollins.
Attendance: 19,023.
Time: 2:20.

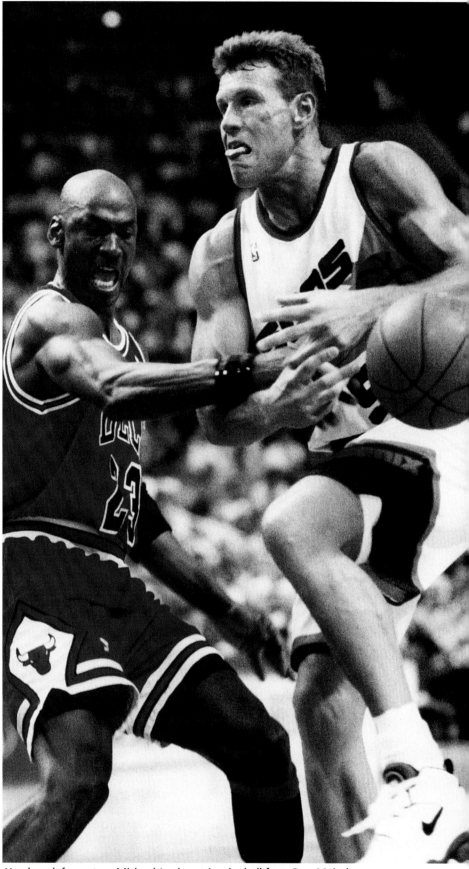

He plays defense, too: Michael Jordan strips the ball from Dan Majerle.

Every loose ball is worth diving for in the NBA Finals, as Mark West and Michael Jordan demonstrate in Game 1.

B.J. Armstrong becomes KJ's nemesis, scoring 16 points and bedeviling the Suns' playmaker on defense.

Richard Dumas gives Scottie Pippen a lesson in offense. Dumas , who scored 20 points, says, "There was no pressure on me."

Charles Barkley and Horace Grant battle on the boards — one facet where the score was about even. The Suns had 42, the Bulls 41.

"I thought I got some good shots," Barkley says after the game. "They didn't go in. I didn't play that well. I guess I'll take responsibility for tonight."

GAME 2

One on one, Charles Barkley played Michael Jordan even in a spine-tingling battle of superstars.

But Barkley could not win a game of one-on-five against the Chicago Bulls. His teammates could not deliver on key plays, and the Suns lost, 111-108, digging themselves into a 0-2 hole.

"Well, we're in the right state for holes," Barkley said. "Right now, we fit in with the Grand Canyon."

The game, in which Barkley and Jordan each scored 42, marked the second straight subpar performance by Kevin Johnson — four points, four turnovers, six assists, six fouls.

But one player's troubles didn't make all the difference. Checked by the Bulls' stifling defense, Phoenix missed nine consecutive shots in the fourth quarter, seeing a 98-96 deficit with 6:02 left grow to 106-98 with 1:33 remaining.

Danny Ainge turned in a strong performance, scoring 20 points and making some last-minute shots to pull the Suns within three points with a minute to go.

But the Bulls executed flawlessly at crunch time. Jordan scored 12 of the Bulls' last 15 points, including 10 straight.

"I know it looks very, very bad," Coach Paul Westphal said of the Suns' chances. "But I'm proud of our players. They played very well, but the Bulls played a super game."

BULLS 111, SUNS 108

CHICAGO

	Mn	FG	FT	Rb	At	PF	St	Tr	Pt
Grant f	36	10-13	4-5	8	2	3	2	1	24
Pippen f	42	5-12	5-7	12	4	2	4	7	15
Cartwright c	13	1-3	0-0	2	0	0	0	0	2
Armstrong g	42	4-9	0-0	4	4	4	1	1	8
Jordan g	40	18-36	4-5	12	9	2	2	5	42
Williams	36	4-7	1-4	1	2	4	1	2	9
King	13	1-4	4-4	2	0	2	1	0	6
Tucker	6	0-2	0-0	1	2	1	1	0	0
Paxson	12	2-3	0-0	1	0	1	0	0	5
Totals		**45-89**	**18-25**	**43**	**31**	**21**	**10**	**16**	**111**

PHOENIX

	Mn	FG	FT	Rb	At	PF	St	Tr	Pt
Barkley f	46	16-26	10-12	13	4	3	1	2	42
Dumas f	17	4-8	0-0	0	0	1	1	0	8
West c	8	0-0	0-0	2	1	2	0	1	0
KJohnson g	32	2-8	0-0	0	6	6	3	4	4
Majerle g	43	4-14	2-2	9	4	1	2	2	13
Miller	25	4-6	0-0	6	2	2	2	2	8
Ainge	29	8-14	1-1	3	4	1	0	2	20
Chambers	26	4-9	1-3	7	3	4	0	3	9
FJohnson	14	1-3	2-2	0	4	3	0	1	4
Totals		**43-88**	**16-20**	**40**	**28**	**23**	**9**	**17**	**108**

FG percentage: Chicago .506, Phoenix .489.
FT percentage: Chicago .720, Phoenix .800.
Three-point shots: Chicago 3-7 (Jordan 2-2, Paxson 1-1, Armstrong 0-2, Tucker 0-2), Phoenix 6-13 (Majerle 3-8, Ainge 3-4, Barkley 0-1). **Blocked shots:** Chicago 7 (S. Williams 3, Grant 2, Pippen 2), Phoenix 12 (Majerle 5, Miller 3, Chambers 2, Barkley 1, West 1).

CHICAGO	28	31	28	24	111
PHOENIX	29	24	31	24	108

Officials: Jake O'Donnel, Joe Crawford and Jack Madden.
Attendance: 19,023.
Time: 2:25.

In what looks like a good wrestling maneuver, Mark West ties up Scott Williams in a battle for rebounding position. The Bulls outrebounded the Suns 43-40.

This collision of superstars is won by Michael Jordan, who eludes Charles Barkley and scores on a reverse layup.

Dan Majerle, upset after the Game 2 loss, says, "If any team can go 0-2 at home and come back to win a series, it's our team."

Charles Barkley encourages Oliver Miller as the Suns struggle in the fourth quarter.

Playing with pain after an injury in Game 2, Charles Barkley gets 24 points and 19 rebounds in a thrilling Game 3.

Richard Dumas gets a step on Scottie Pippen and drives toward the hoop. Dumas scored 17 points and had five rebounds in 24 minutes.

GAME 3

It was a game that woke the echoes from 1976. Garfield Heard, Paul Westphal, John Havlicek move over — the Greatest Game Ever Played now has a sequel.

"This time, the good guys won," said Westphal, who played in the game 17 years ago and coached in this one as the Suns bested the Bulls in triple overtime, 129-121.

Like the '76 game, in which the Boston Celtics needed three overtimes to beat the Suns, 128-126, this one was a dramatic, exhausting test of nerves and will.

Charles Barkley, who injured an elbow in Game 2, fought the pain and came up with 24 points and 19 rebounds. Kevin Johnson exorcised the demons that plagued him in the first two games of the series. He played a playoff-record 62 minutes, scoring 25 and contributing strong defense against Michael Jordan.

It was Jordan, who put up 43 shots to score 44 points, who couldn't get the big ones to fall. Scottie Pippen, who fought leg cramps from the fourth quarter on, was ineffective in overtime.

The Suns did it the hard way, which seems to be the only way they know in the playoffs.

They led by 11 points in the fourth quarter before the Bulls stormed back.

They fell four points behind with 32.6 seconds left in the second overtime, staying alive because Dan Majerle's 20-footer fell with 3.2 seconds left.

Majerle scored five in the third overtime, finishing with an NBA Finals record-tying six three-pointers. And Barkley made the play that broke the backs of the Bulls, scoring after stealing an inbound pass by Stacey King.

"This was the greatest basketball game I ever played in," Barkley said. "It's not about winning and losing; it's about doing the best you can."

SUNS 129, BULLS 121

PHOENIX

	Mn	FG	FT	Rb	At	PF	St	Tr	Pt
Dumas f	24	7-16	3-4	5	1	3	3	1	17
Barkley f	53	9-20	5-9	19	4	5	1	2	24
West c	36	4-7	3-6	5	1	3	0	2	11
KJohnson g	62	11-24	3-4	7	9	5	2	7	25
Majerle g	59	10-17	2-2	7	4	0	2	0	28
Miller	11	1-1	0-0	2	1	4	0	3	2
Ainge	40	2-5	4-4	5	5	4	0	1	10
Chambers	27	5-9	2-2	2	0	2	1	3	12
FJohnson	2	0-0	0-0	0	0	0	0	0	0
Mustaf	1	0-0	0-0	0	0	0	0	0	0
Totals		**45-99**	**22-31**	**52**	**25**	**26**	**9**	**19**	**129**

CHICAGO

	Mn	FG	FT	Rb	At	PF	St	Tr	Pt
Pippen f	56	12-35	2-2	10	9	3	1	4	26
Grant f	45	6-11	1-1	17	1	6	2	2	13
Cartwright c	20	4-12	0-0	3	2	2	1	0	8
Armstrong g	58	10-17	0-0	0	7	4	0	1	21
Jordan g	57	19-43	3-6	9	6	5	2	3	44
Williams	46	2-8	0-0	14	4	3	2	2	4
King	12	0-2	0-0	5	2	0	0	2	0
Paxson	5	1-1	0-0	0	0	3	0	0	2
Tucker	14	1-1	0-0	1	1	3	0	1	3
Walker	2	0-0	0-0	0	0	0	0	1	0
Totals		**55-130**	**6-9**	**59**	**32**	**29**	**8**	**16**	**121**

FG percentage: Phoenix .495, Chicago .423.
FT percentage: Phoenix .710, Chicago .657.
Three-point shots: Phoenix 9-13 (Majerle 6-8, Ainge 2-3, Barkley 1-1, K .Johnson 0-1), Chicago 5-13 (Jordan 3-9, Tucker 1-1, Armstrong 1-3). **Blocked shots:** Phoenix 8 (West 2, Miller 2, Dumas, Barkley, K .Johnson, Chambers), Chicago 6 (Pippen 3, Jordan, S. Williams, King). **Fouled out:** Grant.

PHOENIX	29	29	28	17	4	7	15	129
CHICAGO	29	28	28	18	4	7	7	121

Officials: Darell Garretson, Mike Mathis and Dick Bavetta.
Attendance: 18,676.
Time: 3:20.

Kevin Johnson, his determination fueled by frustration, is fouled by John Paxson on a drive.

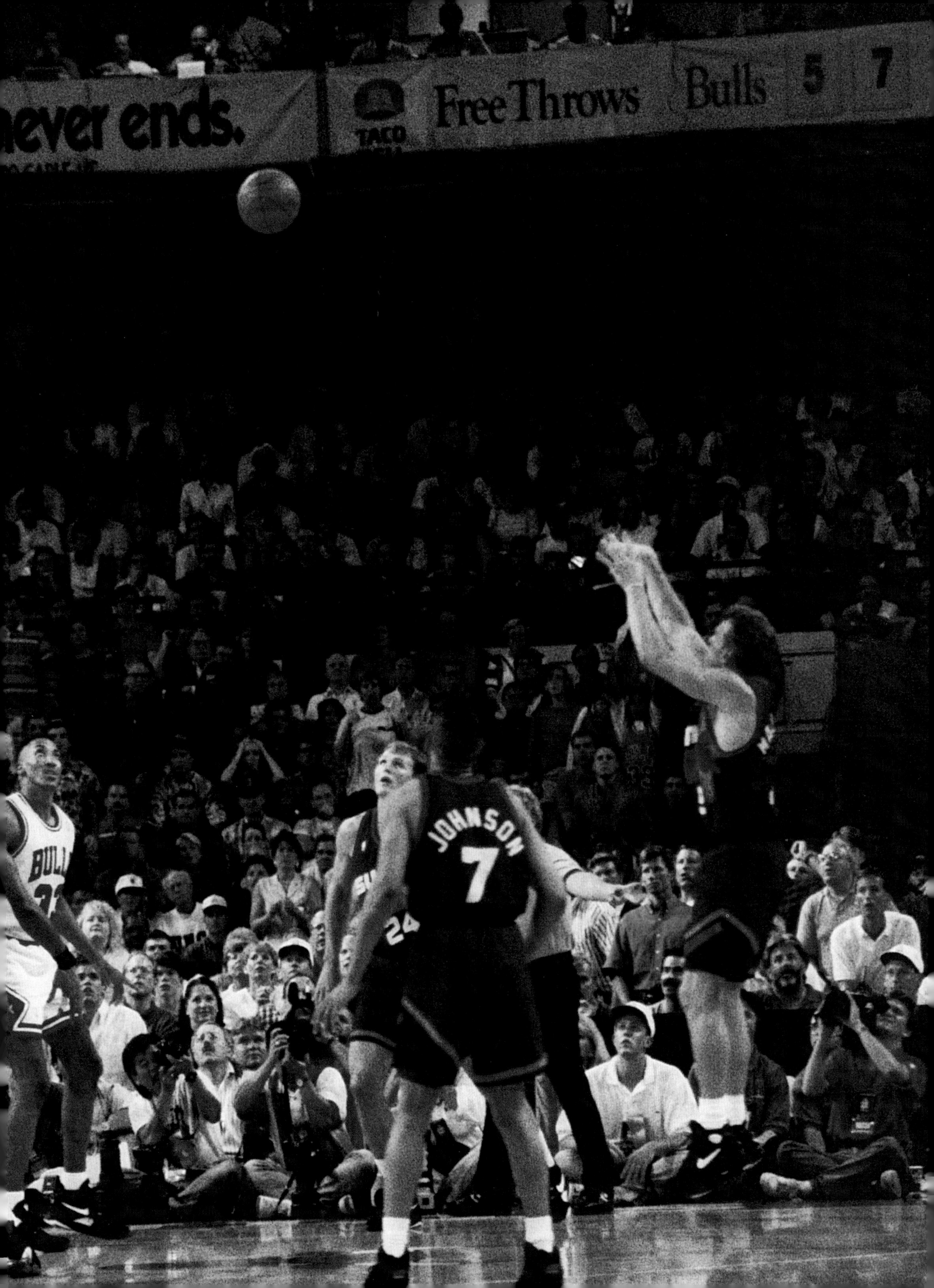
never ends.
TACO
Free Throws
Bulls
5
7
BULLS
JOHNSON
7
24

Dan Majerle's 20-footer with seconds left in the second overtime **(previous pages)** knots the score at 114 and sends the game into its third overtime.

Dan Majerle and Scottie Pippen tangle for the ball. Majerle has the advantage over the Bulls' forward late in the contest as Pippen fights leg cramps.

"It was the greatest game I've ever been associated with. I honestly didn't really care who won and who lost."
CHARLES BARKLEY

"It was a great game to play in but difficult to accept the loss, especially here in Chicago. I don't want to remember the best game I ever played in as a loss."
MICHAEL JORDAN

Sunbelievable! Spirits of '76

Coming soon to a video store near you: "The Greatest Game Ever Played! Part Deux." As sequels go, this one's not bad.

There have been a few changes. For one thing, it was filmed on location in an ancient ruin in Chicago instead of an ancient ruin in Boston.

For another, the only four holdovers from the original cast have roles as winners instead of losers.

Sequels don't as a rule get very good notices and critics may carp that "Deux" doesn't pack quite the dramatic wallop of the original.

But the guys who were in both — Jerry Colangelo, Paul Westphal, Joe Proski and Al McCoy — will tell you the critics are crazy.

"This one's got a much better ending," they insist.

Also, with all due respect to John Havlicek, Garfield Heard and the other stars of the original, a better cast.

And much better subplots.

COMPARATIVELY SPEAKING: June 4, 1976, Game 5, NBA Finals — Boston 128, Phoenix 126, three overtimes.

June 13, 1993, Game 3, NBA Finals — Phoenix 129, Chicago, 121, three overtimes.

Westphal, now the Suns' coach, played in the '76 game, while Colangelo, Proski and McCoy essentially had the same roles in both classics: chief executive officer, trainer and "voice."

As one who covered both games, I offer some comparisons:

Unlike the '76 classic, which featured a mini-riot and a controversial non-call of a Boston request for an illegal timeout, this game was all basketball, albeit somewhat diluted late by fatigue.

Unlike that game, which was played in a sudsy caldron (Beantowners really beered-up) and ended at the ungodly hour of 12:30 a.m., this one was played at room temperature and ended at a normal hour.

NO LACK OF DRAMA: However, the '76 game had the edge in dramatic shots: Havlicek's twisting, wrong-foot bank shot with five seconds left to save the Celts once and Heard's arching 17-footer with no time left to save the Suns once.

For Colangelo, there was a nightmarish "deja-vu all over again" moment Sunday when Scottie Pippen missed a bank shot at the end of the second OT.

"I was lined up with it," Colangelo said, "and it was not only from just about the same spot as Havlicek's but off the wrong foot, too.

"And I thought, 'Oh no. Not again.'"

As is the case in any triple-overtime game, each team dodged quite a few bullets along the way, although this is even more of a figure of speech than usual, since both were so exhausted they were mostly firing blanks in the first two OTs.

You never saw such an assortment of air balls and strange-looking clankers and clinkers.

-Next page

Thrills triple in remake of finals epic

-Previous page

As for those subplots, how about Kevin Johnson, brutalized in the Chicago media after the first two games, coming back with a 25-point, nine-assist, 63-minute effort at one end and a great defensive effort on Michael Jordan at the other?

Or C. (for Courageous) Charles Barkley, playing with a painful right elbow that made every shot agony, delivering 25 points and 19 rebounds, not to mention the steal that sealed the victory?

Or Dan Majerle, who beat Seattle with an incredible eight-of-10 threes, doing likewise unto the Bulls with a scarcely less credible six of eight?

NO CHOICE BUT TO WIN: However, heroics and dramatics aside, the truth is, this would have been an unspeakably bitter game for the Suns to lose.

Not only did they have an 11-point lead with 6:19 to play in regulation, but if you can't beat the Bulls on a night Michael Jordan and Scottie Pippen miss 47 shots between them, then the critics are right: You really don't have any business in the finals.

His Err-ness was a horrendous nine for 27 after intermission, and missed a free throw with 40 seconds left in the second OT that would have given the Bulls a five-point lead.

Ironically, the Bulls suspected putting Johnson on Jordan was some kind of trick and didn't really try to take advantage of the mismatch by posting Johnson up until Jordan's legs were gone and it was too late.

It must also be noted the Bulls did not come ready to play. You could see that early on in their defense, which didn't have nearly as many teeth in it as it did in Phoenix.

The effort they had to expend to catch up in the fourth period ran them out of gas in the third OT — well, out of fumes. Both teams ran out of gas long before the third OT.

What did this game prove? That the Suns have a lot of heart and a lot of talent.

They now also have firsthand evidence the Bulls are human. That even Jordan is not always perfect, that they do get tired and do blow defensive assignments.

Where does this leave the Suns? At the bottom of a steep mountain — but one that doesn't look quite as unclimbable as it did a while ago.

"The Greatest Game Ever Played! Part Trois" anyone?

Joe Gilmartin is a sports columnist for The Phoenix Gazette.

More often than not, Kevin Johnson's relentless drives to the hoop put points on the board. Here, he is called for a foul after charging into Scottie Pippen.

By putting the squeeze on the Bulls, the Suns found new life. Coach Paul Westphal, Oliver Miller and Richard Dumas revel in the moment.

GAME 4 The Bulls needed every one of Michael Jordan's 55 points — and a fateful turnover — to defeat the Suns 111-105 June 16 at Chicago Stadium.

Jordan, stung by comments about his errant shooting in Game 3, came out with a vengeance. He had 33 points in the first half. His total for the game was second only to Elgin Baylor's 61 for the Los Angeles Lakers in 1962.

"The biggest difference in the game is they had Michael and we didn't." Suns Coach Paul Westphal said.

"It was just a magnificent performance. We stopped him a few times, but he also inflicted his will on us a few times."

Down by 13 in the fourth quarter, the Suns clawed back into the game and had the ball with less than a minute left and a chance to tie.

But Scottie Pippen knocked the ball out of bounds as Dan Majerle drove on a two-on-one break. Then the ball slipped out of Kevin Johnson's hands on Danny Ainge's inbound pass, and the Suns' chances went with it.

Jordan drove to the basket, was fouled by Charles Barkley and converted the three-point play.

"When we needed a big basket, I was always there to get that for us," Jordan said. "That's my role."

BULLS 111, SUNS 105

PHOENIX

	Mn	FG	FT	Rb	At	PF	St	Tr	Pt
Dumas f	25	8-11	1-1	1	0	3	1	2	17
Barkley f	46	10-19	12-15	12	10	1	3	1	32
West c	19	3-5	2-2	4	0	6	0	1	8
KJohnson g	43	7-16	5-6	3	4	3	0	3	19
Majerle g	46	5-9	1-3	5	3	1	0	0	14
Miller	14	1-3	0-0	2	1	5	1	1	2
Chambers	23	1-9	5-6	4	0	4	0	1	7
Ainge	21	1-5	0-0	3	2	3	0	1	2
FJohnson	3	2-2	0-0	0	0	2	1	0	4
Totals		38-79	26-33	34	20	28	6	10	105

CHICAGO

	Mn	FG	FT	Rb	At	PF	St	Tr	Pt
Pippen f	44	7-14	0-2	6	10	1	1	6	14
Grant f	37	7-11	3-6	16	2	5	3	0	17
Cartwright c	30	1-4	1-2	5	2	4	0	0	3
Armstrong g	35	4-10	2-2	2	6	2	3	1	11
Jordan g	46	21-37	13-18	8	4	3	0	1	55
McCray	4	0-0	0-0	1	0	0	0	1	0
Tucker	1	0-0	0-0	0	0	0	0	0	0
Paxson	18	2-5	0-0	3	1	2	0	1	6
King	9	1-1	1-2	0	0	3	1	0	3
Williams	14	1-1	0-0	1	0	6	0	0	2
Walker	2	0-0	0-1	0	1	0	0	0	0
Totals		44-83	20-33	42	26	26	8	10	111

FG percentage: Phoenix .481, Chicago .530.
FT percentage: Phoenix .788, Chicago .606.
Three-point shots: Phoenix 3-8 (Majerle 3-5, Miller 0-1, Barkley 0-2), Chicago 3-9 (Paxson 2-4, Armstrong 1-2, Jordan 0-1, Pippen 0-2). **Blocked shots:** Phoenix 3 (Barkley, West, Majerle), Chicago 5 (Grant 3, Armstrong, Williams). **Technicals:** Ainge, Jordan. **Flagrant foul:** Armstrong.

PHOENIX	27	31	23	24	105
CHICAGO	31	30	25	25	111

Officials: Hugh Evans, Bill Oakes and Ed T. Rush.
Attendance: 18,676.
Time: 2:41.

Michael Jordan slips by his defenders (previous page) once again on a drive to the hoop. Horace Grant (above) plays strong defense but Sir Charles comes up with a triple double.

Tempers flare after Danny Ainge takes an elbow. Barkley tries to restrain Jordan from doing anything more than make a pointed remark.

Kevin Johnson tries to avoid the near-constant harassment of Scottie Pippen.

GAME 5

"Save the City" was the pregame rallying cry. With all Chicago — including the police and National Guard — anticipating a "three-peat" and a riot, the Suns canceled the celebration June 18 with a 108-98 win.

They scored early, and often, led by Richard Dumas' 25 points. They played tenacious defense, double-teaming the ball and clogging the middle. And they hung tough as John Paxson's three-pointers helped the Bulls rally from 16 down to take a three-point lead in the second quarter.

"I told Michael (Jordan) at dinner the other night that it was destiny for us to win," Charles Barkley said.

The Suns stayed loose in their fifth win-or-else game of the playoffs. Every time the Bulls got close, someone hit a big shot. Kevin Johnson had 11 points in the fourth quarter and Danny Ainge had eight, including a key three.

Jordan scored 41, but his teammates, except for Paxson, were largely ineffective.

Chicago led the series 3-2 but the Suns had regained the home-court advantage as the teams headed back to Phoenix.

"If we can't win two games at home, then we don't deserve to be world champions," Coach Paul Westphal said.

SUNS 108, BULLS 98

PHOENIX

	Mn	FG	FT	Rb	At	PF	St	Tr	Pt
Dumas f	30	12-14	1-2	5	0	2	1	2	25
Barkley f	42	9-18	6-7	6	6	2	0	1	24
West c	33	2-4	1-2	9	1	3	0	0	5
KJohnson g	41	10-20	5-5	1	8	2	1	4	25
Majerle g	44	3-11	3-4	12	7	1	2	1	11
FJohnson	10	0-2	2-2	1	0	1	2	0	2
Miller	16	3-8	2-2	8	1	4	0	1	8
Ainge	22	3-6	1-2	3	1	1	0	1	8
Chambers	1	0-0	0-0	0	0	0	0	0	0
Mustaf	1	0-0	0-0	0	0	0	0	0	0
Totals		42-83	21-26	45	24	16	6	11	108

CHICAGO

	Mn	FG	FT	Rb	At	PF	St	Tr	Pt
Pippen f	42	8-20	6-8	6	5	5	2	3	22
Grant f	38	0-4	1-4	7	1	3	1	1	1
Cartwright c	14	1-3	0-0	2	2	1	0	1	2
Armstrong g	37	3-8	0-0	2	4	3	0	1	7
Jordan g	44	16-29	7-10	7	7	5	0	2	41
Williams	18	2-4	0-0	5	1	1	0	1	4
Paxson	23	4-5	0-0	3	0	1	3	0	12
King	10	1-2	2-2	0	0	1	0	0	4
Perdue	9	0-2	0-0	3	0	2	0	0	0
Tucker	4	2-2	0-0	0	0	0	0	0	5
Walker	1	0-0	0-0	0	0	0	0	0	0
Totals		37-79	16-24	35	20	22	6	9	98

FG percentage: Phoenix .506, Chicago .468.
FT percentage: Phoenix .808, Chicago .667.
Three-point shots: Phoenix 3-10 (Majerle 2-6, Ainge 1-1, Barkley 0-3), Chicago 8-18 (Paxson 4-5, Jordan 2-7, Tucker 1-1, Armstrong 1-3, Pippen 0-2). **Blocked shots:** Phoenix 4 (Dumas, West, Majerle, Miller), Chicago 4 (Jordan 2, Pippen, K Williams).

PHOENIX	33	21	26	28	108
CHICAGO	21	28	24	25	98

Officials: Joe Crawford, Jess Kersey and Jake O'Donnell.
Attendance: 18,676.
Time: 2:24.

Richard Dumas shows Bill Cartwright and Michael Jordan that he can score, too. Dumas soared to 25 points and five boards.

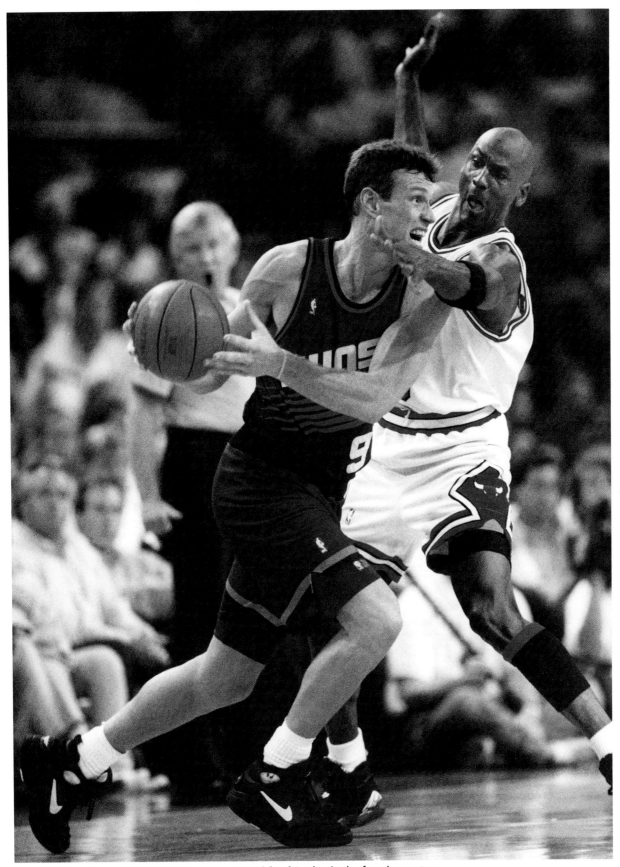

Dan Majerle tries to take it to the hoop against Michael Jordan in the fourth quarter.

Negele Knight (center) and Oliver Miller begin to celebrate as the Phoenix victory draws near.

The scoreboard isn't lying: The Suns are winning, and Dan Majerle and Kevin Johnson are heading back to Phoenix.

The season doesn't end for the Suns: Charles Barkley exults as his team nears a necessary win.

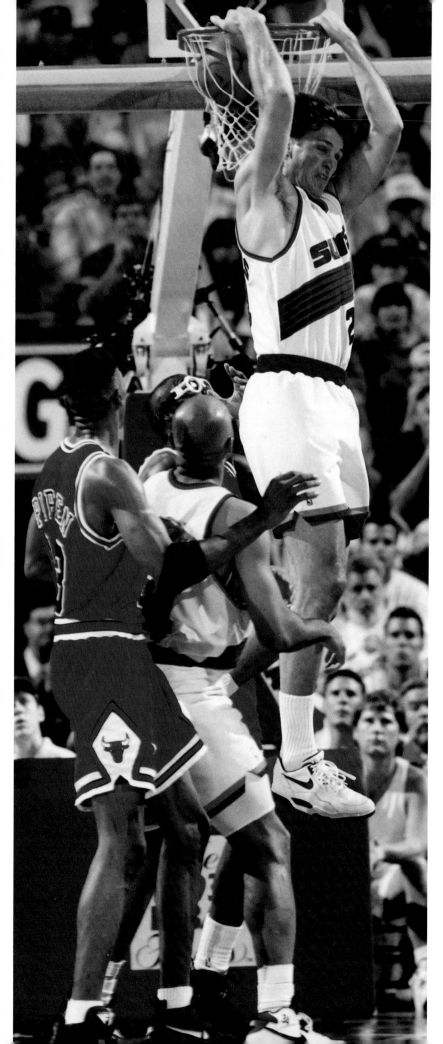

GAME 6

The shot, in flight, is etched in time: John Paxson let it go beyond the three-point line with his team two behind in the closing seconds.

Its aim was true, like a dagger to the heart. The basket gave the Bulls the lead with 3.9 seconds left. Fighters to the end, the Suns could not overcome the final obstacle. Kevin Johnson's last shot was blocked by Horace Grant, and the team from Chicago had achieved its "three-peat" with its fourth victory in the series, a 99-98 win June 20.

Coach Paul Westphal said, "It's something every kid dreams about, and John Paxson got to live that dream out."

"It was quick, so quick, the way it ended," Charles Barkley said. "I mean, you work seven, eight months, and then, wham, it's over."

Chicago made an NBA Finals-record 10 three-pointers in the game, and the Suns were down 10 in the third quarter.

In the fourth, the Suns' defense kicked in, and the Bulls failed to score for 6:09. The Suns took their biggest lead, 98-94, with 2:23 remaining. But they couldn't score again.

"We certainly did it the hard way. We just couldn't hold the Suns down," Bulls Coach Phil Jackson said.

Michael Jordan was named the finals' MVP for the third straight year.

BULLS 99, SUNS 98

CHICAGO

	Mn	FG	FT	Rb	At	PF	St	Tr	Pt
Grant f	33	0-5	1-2	7	3	5	1	0	1
Pippen f	43	10-22	3-7	12	5	3	4	3	23
Cartwright c	26	1-3	0-0	4	1	5	0	0	2
Armstrong g	41	6-10	2-2	0	4	5	0	1	18
Jordan g	44	13-26	4-6	8	7	3	1	3	33
Paxson	22	3-4	0-0	1	1	1	0	0	8
Williams	22	2-7	1-3	7	1	3	0	0	5
Tucker	7	4-4	0-0	0	1	1	0	0	9
King	2	0-1	0-0	0	1	0	0	1	0
Totals		39-82	11-20	39	24	26	6	8	99

PHOENIX

	Mn	FG	FT	Rb	At	PF	St	Tr	Pt
Barkley f	44	7-18	7-10	17	4	5	1	2	21
Dumas f	22	3-8	2-2	3	1	2	0	0	8
West c	20	1-2	2-4	4	1	5	0	0	4
K.Johnson g	46	6-14	7-7	5	10	3	1	3	19
Majerle g	46	7-17	5-6	8	2	3	1	1	21
Miller	14	1-4	2-2	2	0	1	0	0	4
Ainge	30	3-6	1-1	3	2	0	2	2	9
Chambers	12	4-10	4-4	5	0	2	0	0	12
F.Johnson	6	0-3	0-0	0	0	0	0	1	0
Totals		32-82	30-36	47	20	21	5	9	98

FG percentage: Chicago .476, Phoenix .390.
FT percentage: Chicago .550, Phoenix .833.
Three-point shots: Chicago 10-14 (Armstrong 4-5, Jordan 3-5, Paxson 2-3, Tucker 1-1), Phoenix 4-11 (Ainge 2-3, Majerle 2-8). **Blocked shots:** Chicago 2 (Grant 2), Phoenix 9 (Miller 3, West 2, Majerle 2, Dumas, K.Johnson). **Technicals:** Chicago illegal defense.

CHICAGO	37	19	31	12	99
PHOENIX	28	23	28	19	98

Officials: Darell Garretson, Ed T. Rush and Mike Mathis.
Attendance: 19,023.
Time: 2:37.

Tom Chambers does a little showboating for two of his 12 points.

Always quick to socialize, Charles Barkley shares a lighthearted moment with Bulls Coach Phil Jackson. "We never could really get a hold of the Suns," Jackson says after the game. "Not tonight, not in the whole series."

Scottie Pippen soars over Dan Majerle on his way to the basket. Pippen scored 23 points but was shut out in the fourth quarter.

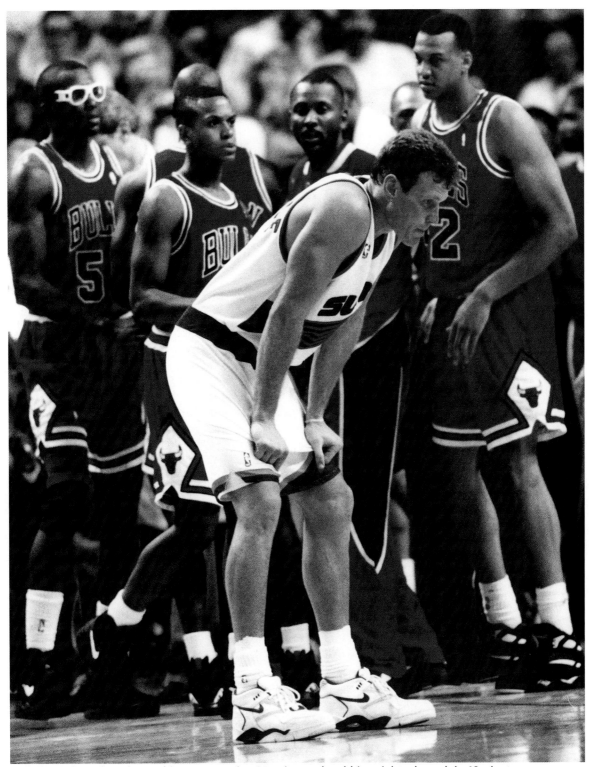

Majerle catches a breather on his way to scoring 21 points and grabbing eight rebounds in 46 minutes.

In a last-second attempt to advance to Game 7, Kevin Johnson **(opposite page)** drives for a shot against Scottie Pippen and Horace Grant, but Grant slaps the ball away. After the final buzzer, a tired Charles Barkley **(above)** walks off the court and toward the Suns' locker room as members of the media swarm the Bulls behind him.

Michael Jordan becomes Dan Majerle's nightmare, blocking Thunder Dan's shot in the fourth quarter of Game 4 of the NBA Finals.

1992-93 RESULTS REGULAR SEASON

Home games in all caps

NOVEMBER

SUNS 111, LA CLIPPERS 105
Portland 100, Suns 89
Suns 102, Utah 91
Suns 108, Minnesota 101
SUNS 117, SEATTLE 108
SUNS 127, SACRAMENTO 111
LA Clippers 111, Suns 107
CHICAGO 128, SUNS 111
SUNS 121, PORTLAND 117
SUNS 121, GOLDEN STATE 107
Golden State 134, Suns 131

DECEMBER

SUNS 109, CHARLOTTE 90
SUNS 103, LA LAKERS 93
Suns 122, Milwaukee 112
Suns 105, New Jersey 100
Suns 110, Charlotte 101
Suns 108, Orlando 107
Suns 122, Miami 118
SUNS 125, WASHINGTON 110
Suns 116, LA Lakers 100
SUNS 106, GOLDEN STATE 104
Suns 111, Denver 96
SUNS 113, SEATTLE 110
SUNS 129, DENVER 88
SUNS 133, HOUSTON 110

JANUARY

San Antonio 114, Suns 113
Suns 106, Houston 104
Suns 111, Dallas 107
Seattle 122, Suns 113
Suns 114, Sacramento 104
SUNS 107, MIAMI 99
New York 106, Suns 103
Cleveland 123, Suns 119
Suns 122, Washington 115
Suns 110, Atlanta 91
Suns 121, Detroit 119
Suns 117, Minnesota 116 (OT)
SUNS 125, SAN ANTONIO 110
SUNS 126, DALLAS 105

FEBRUARY

LA Clippers 112, Suns 108
SUNS 122, MINNESOTA 102
SUNS 132, LA LAKERS 104
SUNS 121, ORLANDO 105
SUNS 122, LA CLIPPERS 100
Suns 122, Golden State 100
Seattle 95, Suns 94
SUNS 110, BOSTON 97
SUNS 131, ATLANTA 119
Suns 105, San Antonio 103
Houston 131, Suns 104
SUNS 113, UTAH 106
CLEVELAND 101, SUNS 94

MARCH

Portland 102, Suns 97
SUNS 125, PHILADELPHIA 115
SUNS 130, SACRAMENTO 122
Suns 109, Dallas 102
Suns 128, Sacramento 108
SUNS 111, GOLDEN STATE 100
SUNS 116, DALLAS 98
NEW JERSEY 124, SUNS 93
SUNS 129, PORTLAND 111
SUNS 127, DETROIT 97
INDIANA 109, SUNS 108
SUNS 121, NEW YORK 92
Suns 120, LA Lakers 105
SUNS 109, MILWAUKEE 103
Suns 110, Philadelphia 100
Suns 113, Chicago 109

APRIL

Suns 118, Boston 114
Suns 110, Indiana 100
SUNS 115, LA LAKERS 114
Suns 123, Sacramento 114
SUNS 98, DENVER 97
SUNS 112, UTAH 99
LA Clippers 111, Suns 104
SUNS 98, MINNESOTA 84
SEATTLE 108, SUNS 102
Utah 110, Suns 101
HOUSTON 111, SUNS 97
Suns 115, Portland 114
SUNS 99, SAN ANTONIO 97
Denver 120, Suns 118

PHOENIX SUNS 1993 PLAYOFF STATISTICS

Player	G	Avg. min	FG-Att	Pct.	3pt-Att	Pct.	FT-Att	Pct.	Pts	Avg. pts
Barkley	24	42.8	230-482	.477	10-45	.222	168-218	.771	638	26.6
West	24	19.5	43-79	.544	0-0	—	28-46	.609	114	4.8
KJohnson	23	39.7	143-298	.480	0-3	.000	124-156	.795	410	17.8
Majerle	24	44.6	134-311	.431	54-137	.394	48-69	.696	370	15.4
Miller	24	21.4	71-121	.587	0-2	.000	31-55	.564	173	7.2
Ainge	24	24.6	64-170	.376	33-80	.413	34-39	.872	195	8.1
Dumas	23	21.7	107-204	.525	0-2	.000	37-49	.755	251	10.9
Chambers	24	15.7	64-165	.388	2-5	.400	44-54	.815	174	7.3
Ceballos	16	11.6	40-70	.571	0-0	——	16-22	.727	96	6.0
FJohnson	22	7.8	22-50	.440	1-3	.333	25-29	.862	70	3.2
Knight	9	3.8	9-16	.563	0-0	——	0-0	——	18	2.0
Mustaf	7	1.4	3-5	.600	0-0	——	0-0	——	6	0.9

Player	Off reb	Def reb	Tot reb	Reb avg.	Ast	Ast avg.	PF	DQ	Stl	Turn	Blk sh
Barkley	93	233	326	13.6	102	4.3	73	0	39	50	
West	36	63	99	4.1	11	0.5	69	2	4	17	
K Johnson	10	52	62	2.7	182	7.9	57	1	35	84	
Majerle	29	111	140	5.8	88	3.7	57	0	33	32	
Miller	33	91	124	5.2	51	2.1	76	0	21	42	
Ainge	20	40	60	2.5	56	2.3	61	0	12	22	
Dumas	36	29	65	2.8	24	1.0	52	0	21	27	
Chambers	23	42	65	2.7	12	0.5	58	0	6	26	
Ceballos	13	24	37	2.3	13	0.8	12	0	5	5	
F Johnson	3	8	11	0.5	17	0.8	26	0	6	7	
Knight	1	2	3	0.3	7	0.8	1	0	0	3	
Mustaf	0	2	2	0.3	0	0.0	0	0	0	0	